Louise Bourgeois' *Spider*

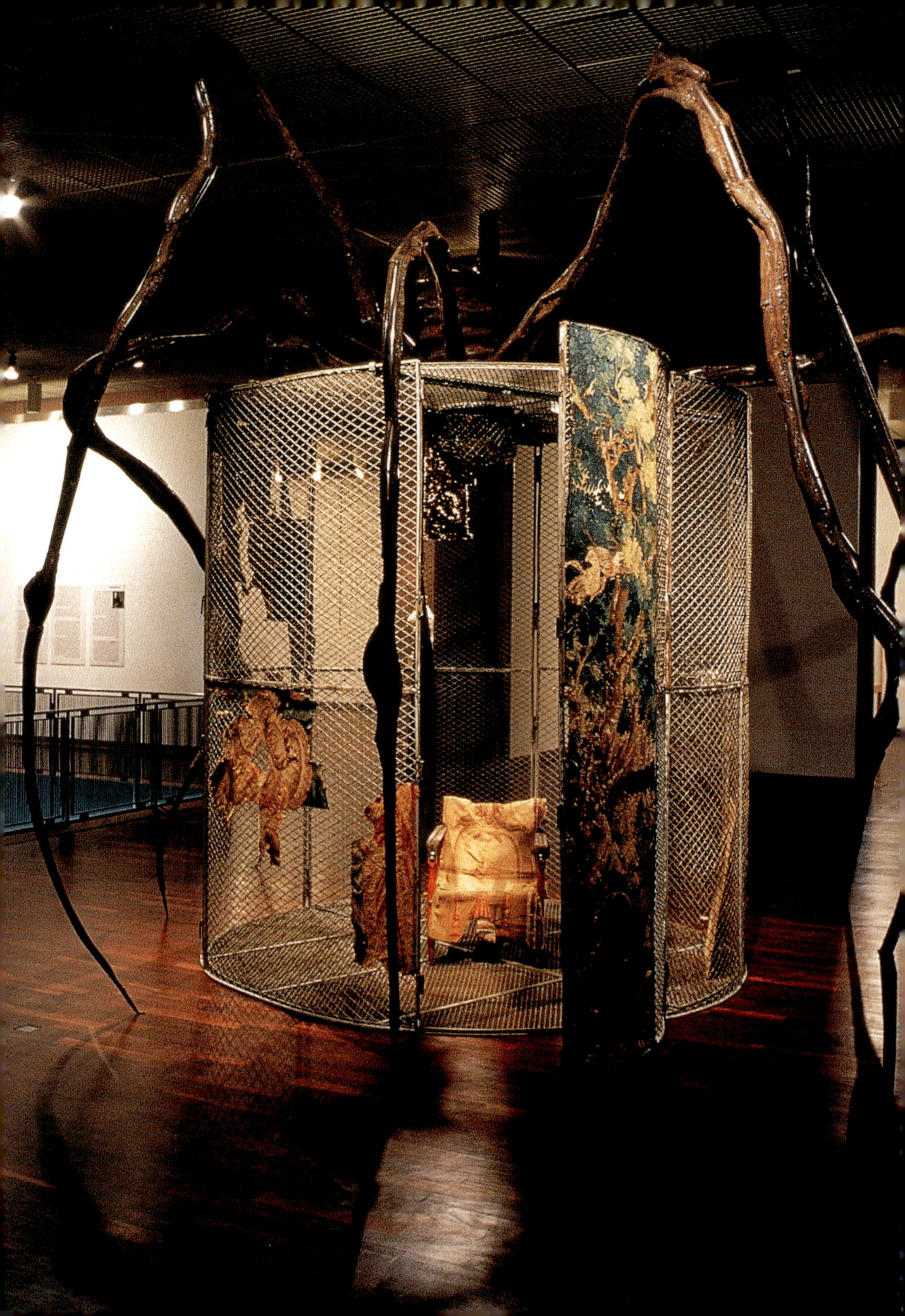

Louise Bourgeois' *Spider*

the architecture of art-writing

MIEKE BAL

the university of chicago press
chicago and london

MIEKE BAL is co-founder of the Amsterdam School for Cultural Analysis, Theory, and Interpretation at the University of Amsterdam and A. D. White Professor-at-large at Cornell University. Her books include *Death and Dissymmetry: The Politics of Coherence in the Book of Judges* and *Quoting Caravaggio: Contemporary Art, Preposterous History,* also published by the University of Chicago Press.

The University of Chicago Press, Chicago 60637
The University of Chicago Press, Ltd., London

Printed in Hong Kong
10 09 08 07 06 05 04 03 02 01   5 4 3 2 1

ISBN (cloth): 0-226-03575-1

Library of Congress Cataloging-in-Publication Data

Bal, Mieke, 1946–
Louise Bourgeois' Spider : the architecture of art-writing / Mieke Bal.
p. cm.
Includes bibligraphical references.
ISBN 0-226-03575-1
1. Bourgeois, Louise, 1911— Spider 2. Bourgeois, Louise, 1911—Criticism and interpretation. I. Spider. II. Title.
N6537.B645 A77 2001
709′.2—dc21   00-011867

This book is printed on acid-free paper.

For August

A WARM WELCOME WITH A WINK

CONTENTS

FIGURES

PREFACE

Louise Bourgeois' installation *Spider* (1997) is one of those works of contemporary art that become familiar while retaining their fascinating strangeness. One of the most striking pieces of Bourgeois' genre series *Cells,* it solicits iconographic reading, while at the same time flaunting the mocking irrelevance of such a reading. It fits no genre or several: sculpture, installation, architecture. It relates to many currents of twentieth-century art, especially sculpture, but also beckons the baroque. Its contents and associations evoke social issues without being reducible to any one of them. It will doubtless become an icon of turn-of-the-century art.

Writing an entire book on this one piece has allowed me to address a great number of issues concerning the methodology of art history and other forms of art-writing, as well as to do full justice to the work itself. This methodological reflection through one work of art has been the driving force behind this text. The integration of close engagement with a single work and the discussion of questions of method lie at its core. Through this integration I have tried to make a simple point as forcefully as I can. The point I want to make is revisionist: I contend that art-writing must sever the all-too-tight connections between disciplinary dogmas, such as those relating to influence, context, iconography, and historical lineage. Instead of following methodological programs, art-writing—I suggest in this book—ought to put the art first. It is from the artworks of contemporary culture, not from the tradition of the disciplines, that methodological procedure and art-historical content must be derived.

Ever since I began writing on visual art, I have been caught up in an ambivalent relationship—not quite "love-hate" but something of that order—with the habits of art-writing. I have never believed in sayings like "a picture is worth a thousand words." Such overvaluations of one medium above another make little sense for a reader of Proust, Mallarmé, and the Hebrew Bible, books in which words, sometimes single ones, *produce* images instead of commenting on them. These valuations seem apologetic, as if the quality of art-writing was doomed from the beginning, simply because words are poor substitutes. Some writers devote thick books to defending this position without noticing how contradictory such endeavors are and without justifying the essentialism on which they are based.

But a profound misunderstanding underlies this position. Writing *about* art is not a substitute *for* the art. Rather than standing in for the visual objects, texts about them ought, in the first place, to lead the reader (back) to those objects. Instead of being a substitute, a good text about art is a *supplement* to it. If all goes well, it unpacks some—and only points to others—of the many facets of that visual work of art. My major dissatisfaction with much—of course, not all—art-writing is that so little is said about what we see and what kind of seeing is involved. When we see with intelligence, the question becomes not where the work comes from, but what the work *is, means,* and *does* in the present time of viewing. In my view, as a literary specialist trained in close reading, the primary lack in traditional art-writing is the absence of a close engagement with the work itself. Close readings of visual works of art are perhaps the most exciting ones. For, instead of demonstrating language's inadequacy, they bring the object closer to the language we need—inevitably—to even be able to think about the visual experience. This essay offers one such close reading for consideration, as a suggested, unassuming, but, in my view, crucial contribution to the traditions of art-writing. Yet, as part of the argument, there is little in this essay that can pass for iconography, connoisseurship, or contextualism.

This might sound preposterously immodest. But in the face of the changing positions of the writer and work of art, respectively, that such an approach entails, I claim that the opposite is true. Whereas in the more traditional approaches to art, works of art are more often than not illustrations to an intellectual argument, here they come first. This is not to suggest that the critic is silenced, hidden behind a false secondariness. No, the overt purpose of this essay is to demonstrate that the closer the engagement with the work of art, the more adequate the result of the analysis will be, *both* in terms of that particular work *and* as an account of the process of looking. Looking with "pictorial intelligence" entails an inevitable revision, based on that work's particularities, of our conceptions of how we look and of what matters in art. This text aims to make a case for such an *attitude*—if that is the right word—toward the process or *work* of art as being the most adequate subject of art-writing.

The interactive principle underlying such an approach feeds into the constantly changing methodology of art-writing. It also undermines any possible attempt to reduce the analysis to a formalistic, descriptive mode. Based on the relational quality of the work, it is by necessity also a principle of openness toward the social as well as the emotional, cognitive, and affective processes that we call, for lack of a better word, aesthetic. But this word can only be used if it is understood, as it was always meant to be, in terms of precisely that process that involves body and mind, viewer and work, in an inextricable mixture. If an account of any such process ends up articulating a different theoretical position, this is precisely because a theoretically strong work of art (one that proposes its own theory) has something to contribute to the way we look at art—at this particular piece, at others "like it," at art in general. In this sense, I propose Louise Bourgeois' *Spider* as a *theoretical object.*

As always, this text could not have been written in isolation. I wish, in brief, to thank all those who were there to discuss *Spider* with me, to start with, Jerry Gorovoy and Pandora Tabatabai Asbaghi, who invited me to write on it. I subsequently wrote this essay while enjoying the auspicious hospitality of the University of Michigan at Ann Arbor in the spring of 1999. My thanks also go to Sherry Marx-Macdonald, who edited the text for me with great care and precision. And as I laid my hand on the last revisions, my grandson August Samuel Voskuil was born. I dedicate this small book to this small boy, for all the joy he will bring.

Amsterdam and Paris, June 2000

ONE

Entrance

> It is only as an image, which flashes up in the moment of its cognizability, never to appear again, that the past can be apprehended.
> WALTER BENJAMIN[1]

Are they sculptures? Installations? Buildings? All and none. Triggers of fantasy and strong statements on art, time, and individual and communal life, Louise Bourgeois' series *Cells* folds such categorical denominations of media and genre into one another.[2] The question of the architecturality of these *Cells* and, by extension, a great number of Bourgeois' works, including works on paper or in oil and the object of this text, *Spider* (1997), imposes itself.[3] From the series or genre of works called *Femme-Maison,* which explores the relationship between body and building, to the overtly built *Cells,* the architectural is present in Bourgeois' art. Present, but never straightforward, and never alone.

Le Corbusier once defined architecture as "the precise and monumental interplay of form within light." All of the terms used in this definition are, without exception, at stake in Bourgeois' *Cells.* But none is taken

1. *Illuminations* 257. Cited by Weigel (1996: 9), who modified the translation.
2. The *Cells,* to which this *Spider* also belongs, are a series of—to date—40 large, uniquely significant works made between 1986 and 2000.
3. All references to *Spider* in this book are to the 1997 installation unless otherwise indicated. *Spider* belongs both to the *Cells* and to a series of works figuring spiders.

for granted, as will become clear below. Architecture is invoked, explored, and contested; it is critically engaged and brought to bear on the sculpture within which it is put forward. I will argue that the mediating term that glues experimental sculpture to the threshold of architecture in Bourgeois' work is "narrative."

It may seem paradoxical to approach the architecturality of Bourgeois' art through the question of the place that narrative and art and art-writing occupy in it. But this is precisely what I propose to do here. For I contend that it is only by tackling this aspect—which, since narrative is the medium of temporality, seems to be the systematic counterpart of architecture, the emblem of spatiality—that her work's sense of architecture can be articulated in terms that go beyond a rigid division of media. As I will argue, it is primarily the architecturality of Bourgeois' work that allows it to overcome the boundaries that usually delimit and confine the different arts.

In order to assess the value of "architecture"—not in any referential, theoretical, or historical sense, but as a concept or key concept, or simply, a key—as an approach to art, the place of narrative in art and the habits around art need to be explored, made explicit, explained. Bourgeois' work is a particularly suitable body of art through which to do this. As I will attempt to demonstrate, her *Spider,* from 1997, one of her most famous recent pieces, is eminently productive as a case in point. For her work in general, and *Spider* in particular, sharpens a paradox inherent in the relationship between visual art and narrative, for which "architecture" offers a solution, or, more modestly, for which architecture is a meeting point. Narrative is a function of Bourgeois' architecture because, uniquely, she infuses form—including the form that informs her work's architecturality—with memory. Not one of her works leaves you indifferent to its personal atmosphere. Yet the memories that inhabit them cannot really be "read," because they are personal, while the works themselves, made public, are no longer uniquely bound to one person's history. Moreover, I submit that on the level of their theoretical import, many of these works—and especially *Spider,* the work central to this essay—all of which are so architectural that they represent, seem to be, or envelop the viewer in houses, also find narrative a trap.

And rightly so. This is why I construe Bourgeois' work, through *Spider,* as both an object and a subject of art-writing—of art history and art criticism. For one thing, the culture within which art functions today is suffering from an overdose of narrativity. Reading *Spider* from this double vantage point is a challenge. How can we both do it justice as a work of art and learn from it, as a theory on, and example of, thought about art? In the sense that they defy the cultural habit of reducing expressions in any medium to the narratives they are purported to convey, Bourgeois' recent works—especially her *Cells*—are dumbfounding. They raise, with particular acuity, a question I find it productive to apply to many of the cultural fields that fall under art history's program: How can visual works of art, specifically sculptures that resist coherent figurative readings, tell stories? And what is the point of attempting to answer such a question anyway? As an example of Bourgeois' work from the last decade—astonishingly varied, dense in meaning, and exuberantly visual, yet difficult to "read" and far from "beautiful"—*Spider* will be examined here through this double question. As it turns out, the answers lie in the realm where sculpture becomes architecture and architecture sculpture. Where these two domains of incompatible scale, volume, and density bounce back on each other, narrative becomes a tool, not a meaning; a mediator, not a solution; a participant, not an outsider.

I will discuss a number of issues pertaining to the cultural status of, specifically, visual narrative and to its function as a cementing force that makes an ever-mobile flipping-over between sculpture and architecture possible. I will argue this in close dialogue with Bourgeois' well-known *Spider.* Gigantic and fragmented, enigmatic and suggestive, this sculpture or installation solicits, yet resists, a narrative approach. It raises the question of the relationship between architecture and narrative with more specificity than most of Bourgeois' other works from the same period, for it is situated within two different series, each concerned with home, body, and memory, but each engaging that cluster of preoccupations in totally different ways.

The forty works that—to date—comprise the *Cells* are, perhaps, best characterized as sculptural installations with a sense of *habitat* that makes them architectural. Each *Cell* is different, self-contained, an autonomy, to which the concept, form, and even the title of the series bear witness. But, despite this proclaimed completeness, the concept of each work is so specific and so consistently maintained that its most characteristic aspect—architectural self-containment—enforces the acknowledgment that what we have here is really a series.

Photographs of most of the *Cells* have been superbly published and thoroughly discussed and analyzed as a series in Rainier Crone and Petrus Graf Schaesberg's book, *Louise Bourgeois: The Secret Life of the Cells* (1998), which ought to be considered as a background for the present essay.[4] In this essay, I will consider the *Cells,* hence, also *Spider,* as conceptually self-reflexive. That is to say, their concept makes a statement about their art, stipulating that it hinges between sculpture and architecture, a position that in turn

4. I will try to avoid overlap with this in-depth study, an attempt that entails sacrificing aspects of *Spider* that would otherwise require commentary.

hinges on ambivalence toward narrative. In other words, the *Cells* are, among many other things, richly theoretical in their conception and impact—so much so that the first word that came to mind when I was groping to grasp their impact was *theoretical object.*

As I have argued elsewhere, this term refers to works of art that deploy their own artistic and, in this case, visual, medium to offer and articulate thought about art.[5] Here, I wish to make the most of this notion as a guideline for art-writing. My goal is to present not so much a method as an *attitude.* Looking at art from this attitude does not entail "applying" art-historical theory to the work, which puts the act of looking itself under erasure, but rather looking *at* art in the sense of looking *to* art for an understanding of what art is and does. To the extent that I construe *Spider* as a theoretical object, then, this essay is as much about my approach to that work as it is about the work itself.

But *Spider* is not only one of the *Cells.* It also belongs to an ensemble of works here called *Spiders,* which have been less systematically studied as a series. This series consists of a large number of drawings, sculptures, and installations, each representing a huge spider, sometimes in combination with a small one, hovering over a page, a wall, a ceiling, a room, and here, in the case of *Spider,* a cell. Although less studied, these *Spiders* have produced a different kind of text, one that it is more difficult to call critical (although for me criticism is one of its most important functions): literary narrative.[6]

5. In *Reading "Rembrandt,"* I theorized about this aspect of visual art in terms of propositional content. In *Quoting Caravaggio: Contemporary Art, Preposterous History,* I argued that the term *theoretical object* is better suited to foregrounding both the theoretical thought and the visual articulation of that thought in visual objects. The term *theoretical object* is related to the term *meta-painting;* see Stoichita 1997. As far as I know, this term was first discussed at length by Louis Marin and Hubert Damisch in a series of two colloquia at Urbino in the late 1980s. Krauss (1990) speaks about it on the basis of these discussions. Careri (1985) also makes excellent use of the concept.

6. Marie Darrieussecq, *Dans la maison de Louise/Louise's House,* bilingual edition, *hors catalogue* (1997).

The most frequently discussed aspect of the *Spiders*—the mood of the past they convey—is usually talked about in terms of quotations by the artist. The *Spiders* seem to resist critical analysis. It therefore seems fitting that the most extensive commentary on them takes the form of a literary, fictional narrative. They are intensely figurative, hair-raisingly strong in their affect on the viewer, and almost compulsorily narrative. How can you see a big spider and not go back to childhood curiosity, comfort, or terror, indeed, to actively experiencing those feelings?

Unlike the *Cells,* the *Spiders* do not invoke architecture directly, either through their form or their figurative meaning. Yet through the narrativity that inheres to their figurativity and their appeal to mood, they invoke the home, which is where the memories of spiders belong and where little children spin their dreams out of spiders and their webs, webs that catch and enfold whatever comes their way. Moreover, the legs of spiders, blown up on a Bourgeoisian scale, are sturdy columns, supporting the weight of the body and its descendants. Through sheer aggrandizement, they become the skeleton of a house. Thus they join the *Cells* in their endeavor to build a sense of habitat. Having become architectural in size, they become architectural in essence; the body is a building. Size alone can do that. Or can it? The building is a body. Here, memory comes in, spinning the stories that allow the spider to grow big enough to be a building.

So why the centrality of *Spider?* A theoretical object with a strong narrative appeal to create "homeness": what else can I do but try to understand, on its own terms and by thinking about narrative, what this work has to say and do? On its own terms, mind you; and that prior decision, however obvious it may appear, is not easy to live up to when narrative comes into play. Narrative is centrifugal; it entices you to spin off, develop strands that move away from the center of attention, from the work of art, like so many silvery threads that run outward from the spider in her web.

But why a single work in the first place? When confronted with an oeuvre as extensive as Bourgeois', even a study of only her recent work requires rigorous limitation. The limitation to a single work, in combination with wider claims regarding Bourgeois' work, visual art, and art-writing, is in a sense a "willful misreading" (Bloom 1973). This gesture of singling out one work is an attempt to redirect art-writing to the art it writes about but too often subordinates and subjects to the derivative status of illustration of the art-writer's argument. In defiance of the predominance of overviews, which all too often peter out into biographism, I wish to approach Bourgeois' oeuvre through a close engagement with just one of her works—without in the least claiming to give a comprehensive analysis of even this piece.[7] For the duration of this writing, *Spider* will be my home.

Having seen this installation in two recent exhibitions, it seems to me eminently suitable as a means of questioning the predominant mode of discussing art in general and Bourgeois' work in particular, namely, through the narratives about it.[8] But, although

7. It is as a consequence of one of the most baffling features of Bourgeois' work in general that my analysis of this installation in particular cannot be taken to "stand for" or represent her work as a whole, except to the extent that *Spider*'s very complexity *is* representative of it. Nor can my analysis be considered comprehensive even of this single piece, because of another major feature of her work. The strong impact on the viewer makes my own participation in the construction of the analysis not only inevitable but also—paradoxically—necessary if I am to do it justice.

8. I saw *Spider* in the Centro Cultural de Belém, Lisbon, in August 1998 and in the Serpentine Gallery, London, in January 1999. These were two widely different experiences. The impact of an exhibition space and its neighboring works in a specific show is both important and difficult to analyze. A significant feature of a work seems to be its ability to offer permeability to the dividing line between generalizations about a durable object and such contingencies as installations entail. Yet writing about that aspect seems to put my readers at a disadvantage. It is precisely that temporal and spatial existence in the world that characterizes the experience of this work. That experience cannot be fixed in writing or in photography. On issues of exhibition, see my book *Double Exposures*.

typical of Bourgeois' work, questioning common practices is never a significantly relevant purpose in itself, neither for art, nor for writing about art, including my own. Perhaps the strength of her art, and its appeal to me in my attempts to understand how to write about art more adequately, comes from her firm determination to do something with whatever she is critical of. Blowing up those cultural habits that clog thinking from within, this artist merrily goes on after a decisive turn, wasting no time in sitting down with negative conclusions. I wish to learn something of a wider cultural importance from this attitude. In other words, I seek to understand from it, taking up the work's specific effectivity, its *work.* This work is performed in the tense and intense relationship between narrative and architecture. *Spider,* then, stops narrative, as the sloth of art-writing, in its tracks, while at the same time proposing a conception of *visual* narrative that counters the reductionism inherent in the common mode of art-writing.

In short, this essay departs from the following view: Where the *Cells* seem to defy the notion of narrative, the *Spiders* seem to impose it. And whereas the late recognition of Louise Bourgeois as one of the most significant sculptors of the twentieth century has led to a flurry of art-historical and mostly biographical narratives, her work's resistance to attempts to reduce it to either type of story disturbs any comprehensive reading of it and of the surrounding—perhaps obscuring, and at any rate distracting—narratives. To understand *Spider,* therefore, it seems imperative to understand narrative and its persistent presence in writing about art. For it is from beneath the dust gathered by narrative compulsion that I would like to explore the way this work does not *tell* a story but *builds* one, a different one—but one that, in a multiplicity of ways, *matters.*

TWO

> An image is that in which the has-been comes together in a flash with the Now to form a constellation.
> WALTER BENJAMIN[1]

Description Shipwrecked

First, the point of the question about narrative: Why ask the question of narrative's relevance in the face of the stubborn muteness of architectural sculpture? And why ask it in relation to *Spider?* It seems so much more in line with the idea of visual discipline to simply describe that work. So let me try to do that first.

The following description was drawn from my notes of a first viewing of *Spider* in Lisbon in 1998. It serves a number of purposes here. First, it stands in as a humble supplement to the photographs included in this volume, proposing, together with them, a poor substitute for the visual experience the readers of this book can no longer have. This basic lack, inherent in any criticism of *Spider* that comes after the fact of the visual experience, can only be accepted. But whereas this lack must be acknowledged beforehand, its theoretical inevitability will come to the fore as I proceed. Second, my description will serve as the ground or perhaps fabric through which the discussion of the different narrative modes presented below

1. From Benjamin's description of the dialectical image (Weigel 1996: 69).

will gain a minimum of relief.[2] Third, and more specifically, the description's very limitations will offer some insight into the functioning of the narrative motor in the present of viewing, which I will claim helps in understanding the kind of "virtual reality" that, in my interpretation, Bourgeois' *Spider,* as theoretical object "theorizes," as sculpture "embodies," and as building "houses." In this respect, my description is an intertext of a particular kind. Written after and on the basis of *Spider,* it follows the work, while as an introduction to it for readers who don't know it firsthand, it precedes it. In this sense, therefore, my description is, quite literally, *preposterous.* My interventions in the description—indeed, my incapacity to limit myself to description because of narrative's overruling power—can be seen as examples of the way the visual machine enforces the subject's participation in the very undoing of the description. For these reasons, my description is provisional and itself subject to analysis; hence, its graphic distinction.

Spider, 1997. Steel and mixed media, 175 x 262 x 204 in. (444.5 x 665.4 x 518.1 cm) Cheim & Read, New York

At first sight: a round cage, about 4.5 meters in diameter and 5 meters high. Woven steel—sturdier than chicken wire—in sections of about 1 meter. Inside is a sitting-room chair, with a fragment of old woven tapestry lying on it. Correction: at first sight, this structure is dominated by a gigantic bronze spider looming over it. In

2. Not at all claiming a naïve spontaneity of visual experience as the *fabula* of this account, I have not rearranged my notes, which were detached. Instead I have contented myself with shaping sentences out of them, in the fashion of the "secondary elaboration" that Freud rightly claims informs any narrative given in the wakened state of a dream experienced during sleep (*The Interpretation of Dreams*). Whereas this elaboration—this description—is therefore inevitably secondary, it is still, to stay within the Freudian framework, preanalytical, preceding as it does the "free associations" that bring the work of censorship—through displacement, condensation, and visual elaboration—to the fore.

order to see the cage and its elements, one has to dare to confront the spider, to approach the cage between her legs.

The spider is enormous, dramatically challenging scale and the human body's tendency to be its measure. The legs are thick, yet like a ballerina's: they stand on fine points of needle-sharp "toes." The spider's body coincides with the inside, the very center, of the cell. Due to the height of the legs and yet their slender shape, it is not easy to determine where I, as a viewer, stand.

On one side of the outside of the cage a fragment of tapestry is affixed in which antique architecture is represented. This representation of architecture is quite emphatic: the forms in the woven *trompe-l'oeil* are strikingly square, representing linear perspective extending to the left. The squareness seems introduced as a counterpoint against which the round form of the *Cell* agitates.

From the middle of this piece of tapestry, a fragmented woman looks at us (fig. 1). Part of her middle body, from chin to legs, is missing; the missing part has an S-shape. Her legs are crossed, with one of her feet extending to the lower right corner of the fragment. Her right arm is extended upwards, to pull a represented fabric through an iron ring mounted on a wooden block in the ceiling, as if she is decorating the room, while she, as a woven figure in a tapestry, is herself a decoration. This decorating activity is foregrounded by another ring, which already has the bow in it that this fabric may be expected to take the shape of in the near future.

Over this piece of fabric, the enormous spider's leg that is nearest to it curves back to the fabric, duplicating in three-dimensional space the S-shape of the missing part of the woman's body. This leg is the only one that goes back to the cage and stays there. Of the seven legs, the other six bend toward the cage, in a variety of curves, then at the last moment, hover or recede. All seven legs are clearly lively, contributing to the counterpoint of the ancient, woven architecture: they embody antiregularity.

At the height of the spider's "knee" (really heel), two pieces of bone (emptied of marrow) are inserted next to each other into the spaces between the woven steel threads, just below the upper edge of the lower panel. Bone from the grave, bone from soup-making in the kitchen. Death and life in one. Bone with a hole in it, where the marrow once was; solid matter, and yet just a frame around emptiness (fig. 2).

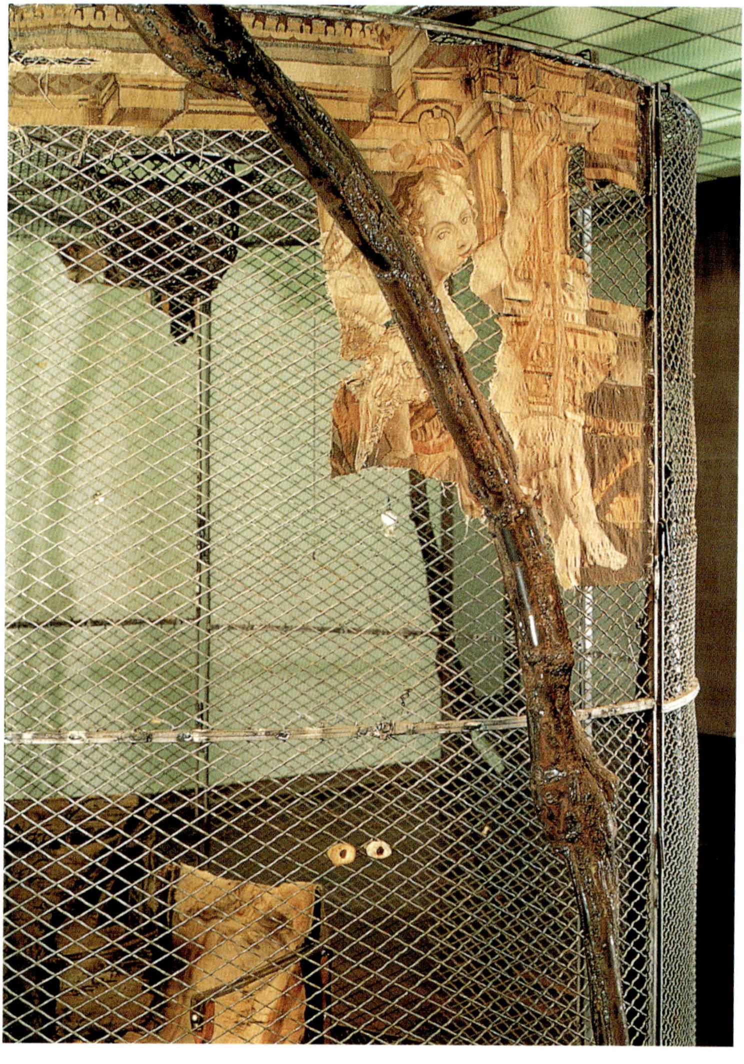

FIGURE 1 Louise Bourgeois, *Spider* (detail: antique architecture with female figure), 1997, steel and mixed media, 175 × 262 × 204 in. Courtesy Cheim & Read, New York. Photograph: Marcus Schneider

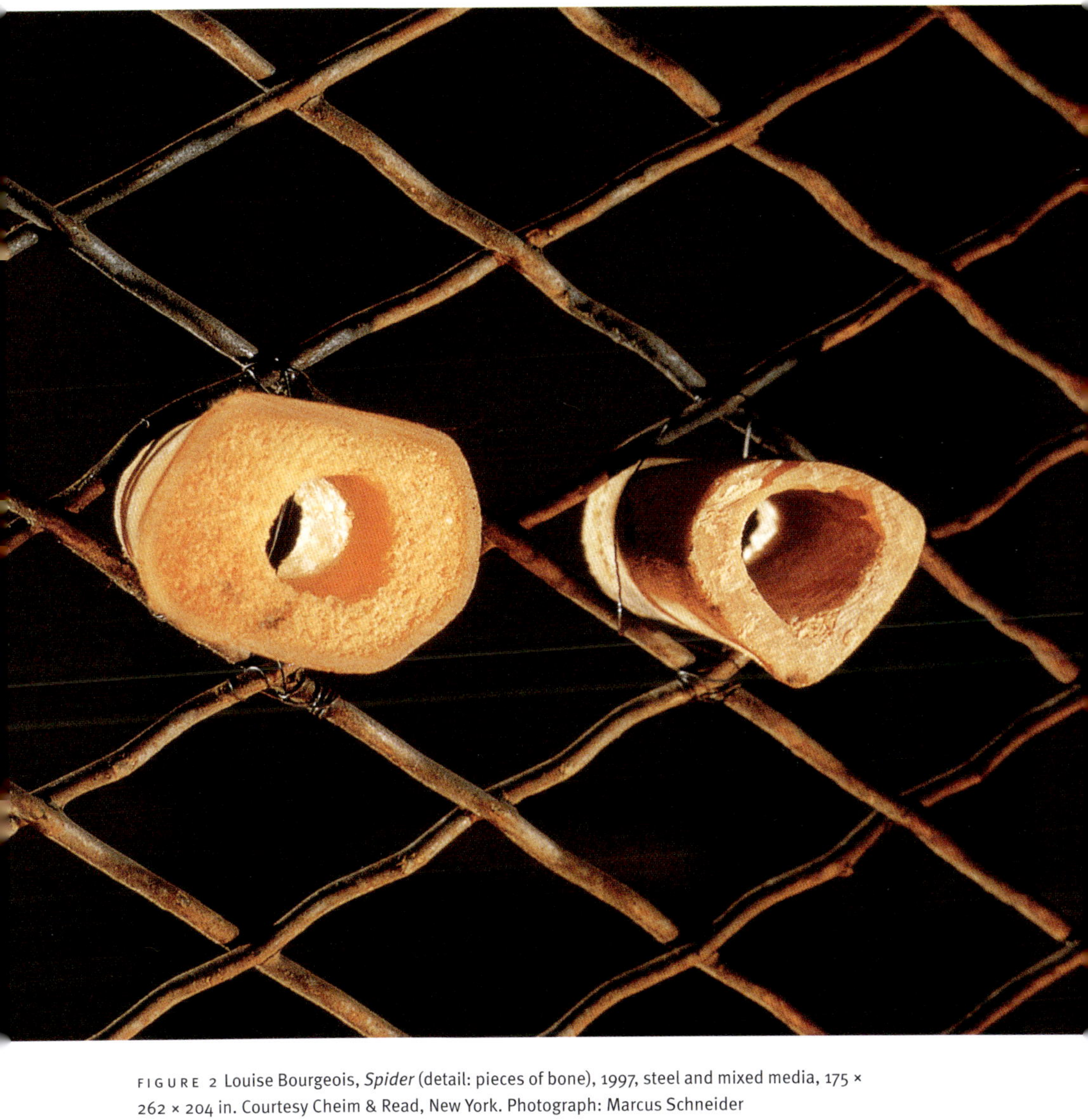

FIGURE 2 Louise Bourgeois, *Spider* (detail: pieces of bone), 1997, steel and mixed media, 175 × 262 × 204 in. Courtesy Cheim & Read, New York. Photograph: Marcus Schneider

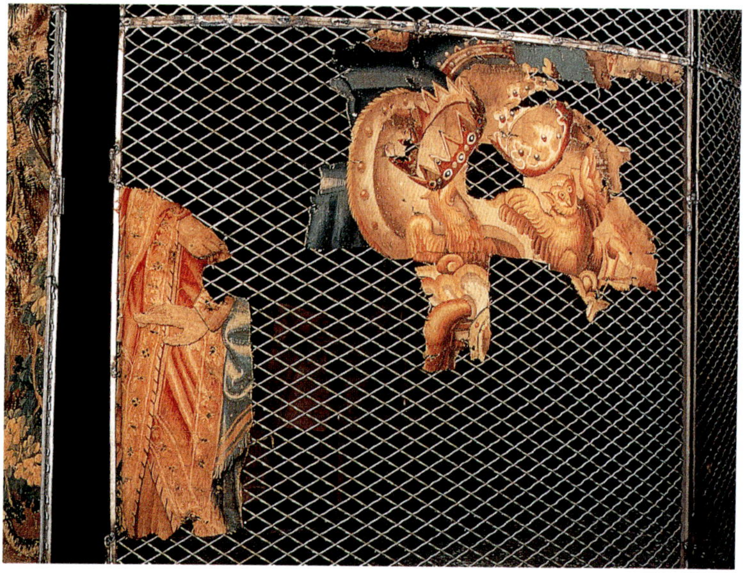

FIGURE 3 Louise Bourgeois, *Spider* (detail: owl and other figures), 1997, steel and mixed media, 175 × 262 × 204 in. Courtesy Cheim & Read, New York. Photograph: Marcus Schneider

More to the left, another fragment of fabric is mounted, facing the back of the chair. This fragment depicts crowns, an owl flying upwards, decorative curls, a blue sky. To the left, at the opening of the door that is ajar, a bit lower than the previous fragment, another, showing what might be the robe of a church dignitary and bits of other figures. The costume displays a powerful position but the figures have no heads, no faces. The only face is that of the owl (fig. 3).

My gaze wavers from these fragments on the outside wall of the cage to inside the cage, where a chair stands so alone (fig. 4). The chair in the cage is quite ordinary, like a director's chair, but it is made to look historical, almost like a throne, by the fabric thrown over it. Not really: the historicizing look is theatrical, overtly presented as fake, just a layer. The part hanging down has tassels. Or does it? The tassels are not real, only flat representations of tassels. Located at the chair's genital

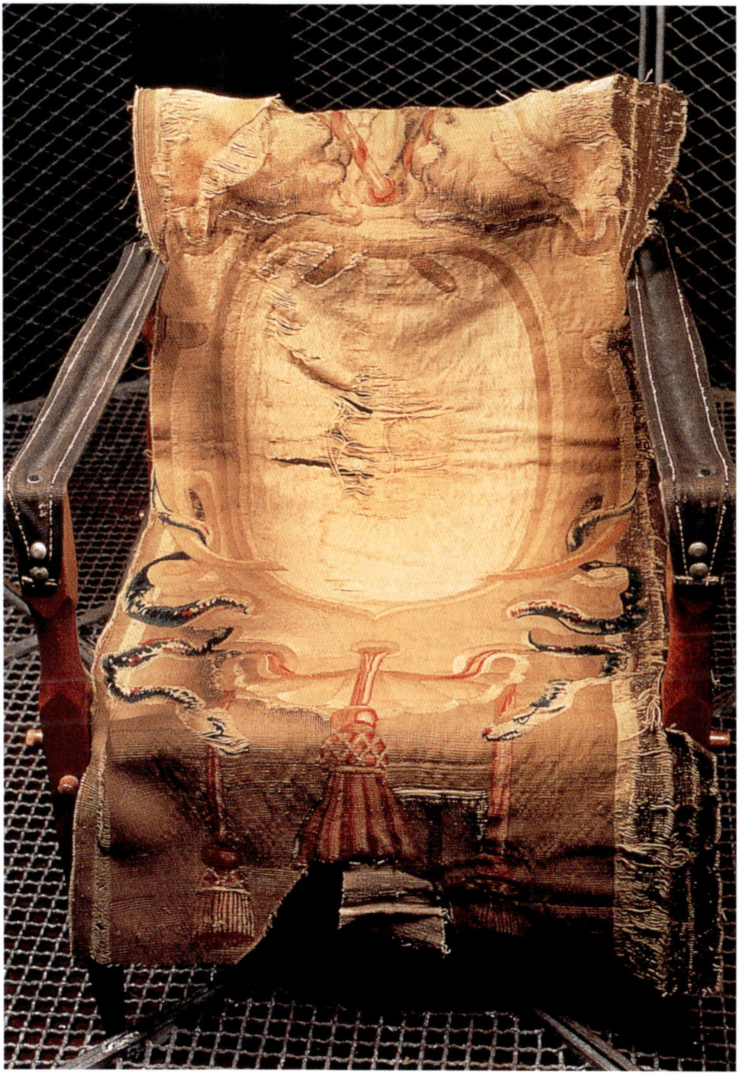

FIGURE 4 Louise Bourgeois, *Spider* (detail: chair), 1997, steel and mixed media, 175 × 262 × 204 in. Courtesy Cheim & Read, New York. Photograph: Marcus Schneider

area (if the chair were a body), the middle tassel seems to be poking fun at the body whose ambition it is to sit there and direct this multiply fictitious play. The snakes threaten to spoil the fun.

From here to the left, still inside the cage, a tapestry panel leans against the wall. Here we can see a sandaled foot, a calf, a lower leg, walking. Some thin grass, flowers (fig. 5). The scene is set outside, although inside the cage. It faces inward, representing the outdoors as inwardly as in a dream. Across from it another fragment mounted on a plank looks back. The lower body of a *putto* whose smile we can only imagine. He lifts his left leg, displaying the gaping hole between his legs, where scissors have exercised censorship in yet another past. The woven steel of the cage's wall behind the figure unwittingly offers a cross, crossing out what was there and foregrounding the act against the body (fig. 19).

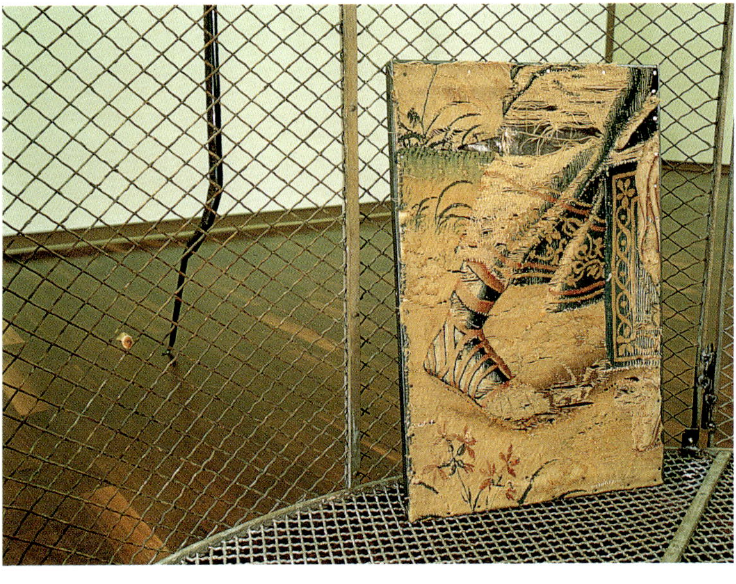

FIGURE 5 Louise Bourgeois, *Spider* (detail: sandalled foot), 1997, steel and mixed media, 175 × 262 × 204 in. Courtesy Cheim & Read, New York. Photograph: Marcus Schneider

The door behind the chair is covered, for about two thirds of its width and from top to bottom, with a tapestry representing a wooded landscape: trees, leaves, plants, birds. It looks idyllic, but at the bottom a swan is turning its head to face a monstrous snake with a gaping mouth. Looking back, the peacefully flying birds seem to be in flight, escaping the primal danger of the millennial snake (fig. 6). Since this scene is affixed to the cell's door, which is open, the holes in the fabric seem to facilitate the transmission of this danger, facing outward, to the inside of the cell.

This moment is crucial. The door is ajar; the cell no longer closes off. Threat is no longer only outside the cell. The spider's legs cannot protect: already, the walls are only bars, imprisoning but not protecting; the door is already opened to the outside, to the snake who is looking at me. And then I see the key, hanging there for everyone to grab. Or just to see?

Next to the door on the lower panel is a small bone, not stuck between the bars but hung on a thread to balance inside, against the steel, but detached from it. Why hanging? At the dividing line between this panel and the next, three small glass cupping jars (the kind that were used to draw poison from the back of the infirm), upside down as if drying, stand on short pins (fig. 7). A bit higher, above the middle of the upper panel, a key hangs inside the cage. A bit to the right of it, still higher up, another bone, a bit larger, is sewn to the steel. Here and there I now see more of those small bones.

The panel of fabric standing inside, on the cell's floor, has a bit of tapestry on its outside, a Pompeian still-life with a black background, a bit of architectural *trompe-l'oeil*. On the left, behind the chair, is a curly architectural decoration, a bird sitting on a ring, with a small fragment on top of it. On the bottom, inside, a small piece mounted on a steel plate. A hole has deliberately been pierced through both fabric and steel. The steel plate is leaning on the ground. On its inside, a *putto*, leaves, and fruit recall the idyllic-yet-threatening outside.

Where the panels meet, inside, on a hook, is a black rubber body, with a shape similar to the pink one in "In Respite," exhibited in the same show, in the Serpentine Gallery in London, sharing its space. The black body has big needles stuck into it, brooches, a bunch of medals (fig. 8).

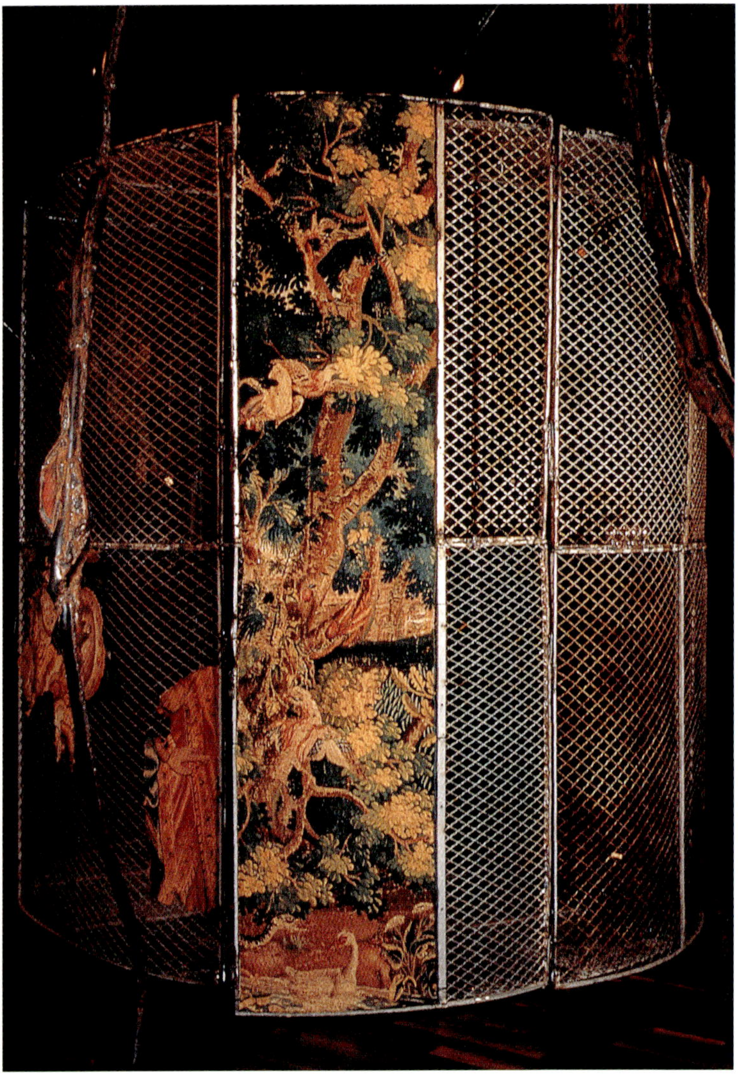

FIGURE 6 Louise Bourgeois, *Spider* (detail: millennial snake), 1997, steel and mixed media, 175 × 262 × 204 in. Courtesy Cheim & Read, New York. Photograph: Marcus Schneider

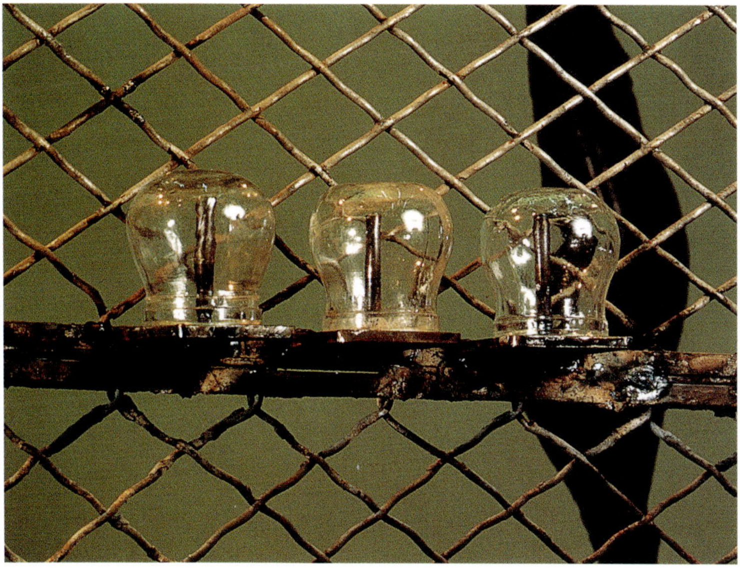

FIGURE 7 Louise Bourgeois, *Spider* (detail: three glass jars), 1997, steel and mixed media, 175 × 262 × 204 in. Courtesy Cheim & Read, New York. Photograph: Marcus Schneider

The spider covers the top of the cell. But once you get used to it, the scale makes the legs turn into columns whose function as protective guards you don't respect any more. The smallness of some of the objects entices you to come closer, so close that the spider loses its wholeness. The scale changes: the cell becomes a large, almost empty room, the spider legs outside it recede into a background, behind my back. Don't turn around.

Inside hang chains with perfume bottles, a medal, a watch. Especially the perfume bottle leads me back in time, accompanied by the imagined ticking of grandfather's watch (figs. 9 and 10). Which secret lover or lost child of another century is hidden by scale and disclosed by the opening of that tiny locket (fig. 11)? The middle of the cell, its ceiling, has the gigantic eggs in a basket, which is also the body of the spider, making her female, motherly (fig. 12). But this basket is not as central for the

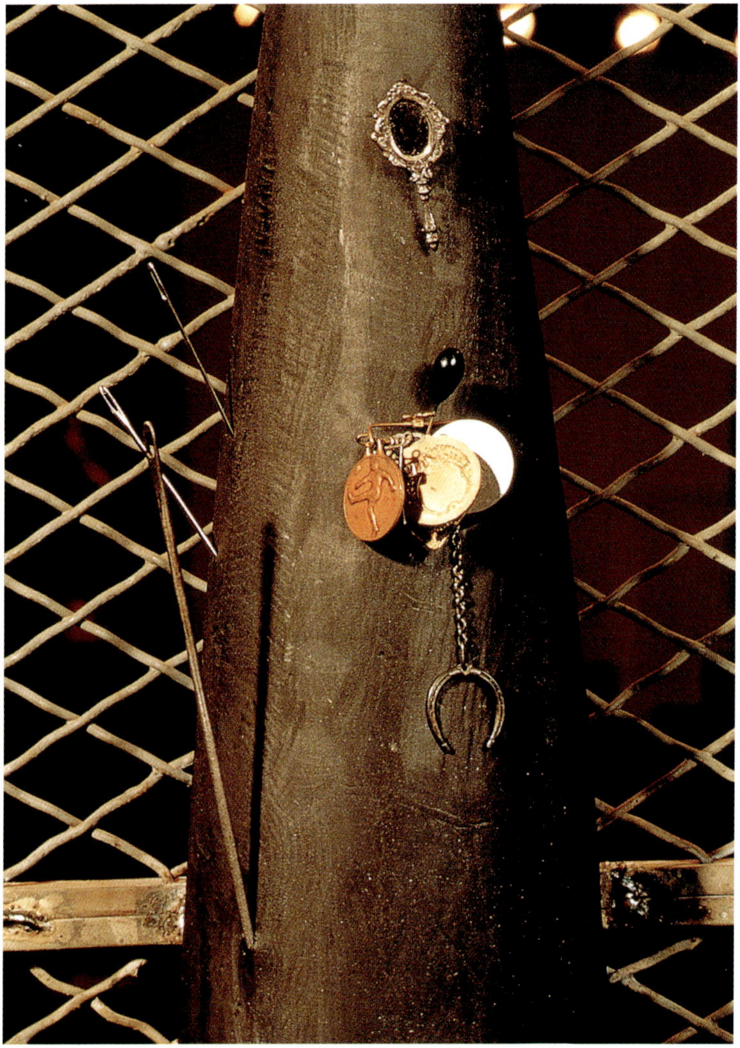

FIGURE 8 Louise Bourgeois, *Spider* (detail: black body with brooches and medals), 1997, steel and mixed media, 175 × 262 × 204 in. Courtesy Cheim & Read, New York. Photograph: Marcus Schneider

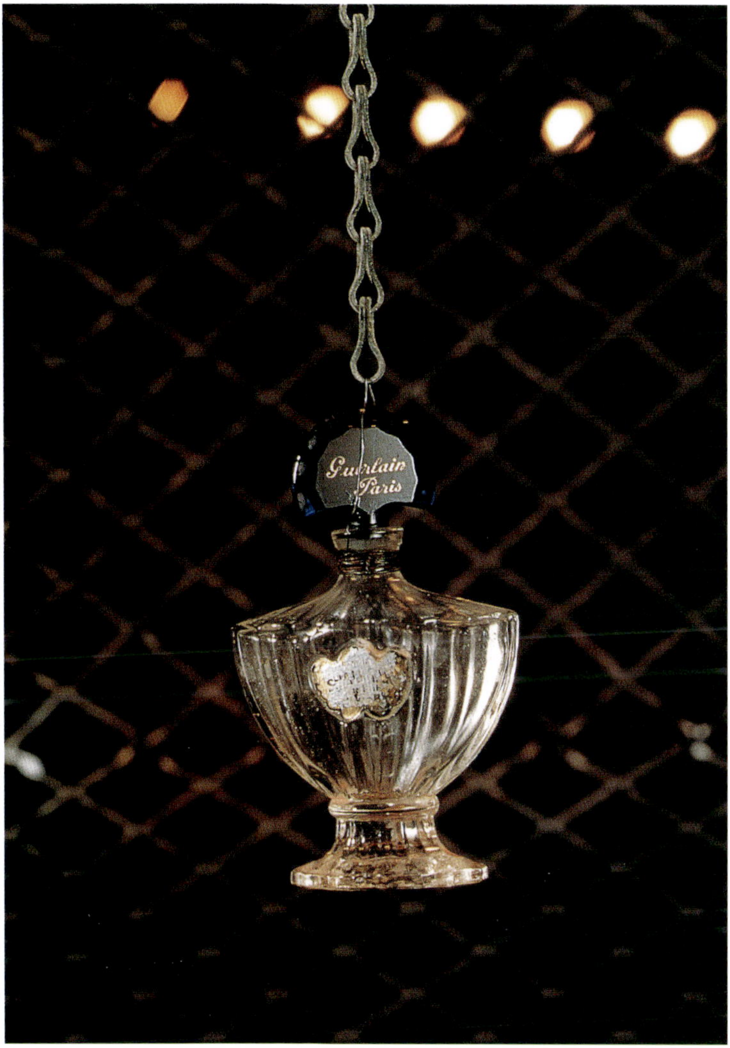

FIGURE 9 Louise Bourgeois, *Spider* (detail: perfume bottle), 1997, steel and mixed media, 175 × 262 × 204 in. Courtesy Cheim & Read, New York. Photograph: Marcus Schneider

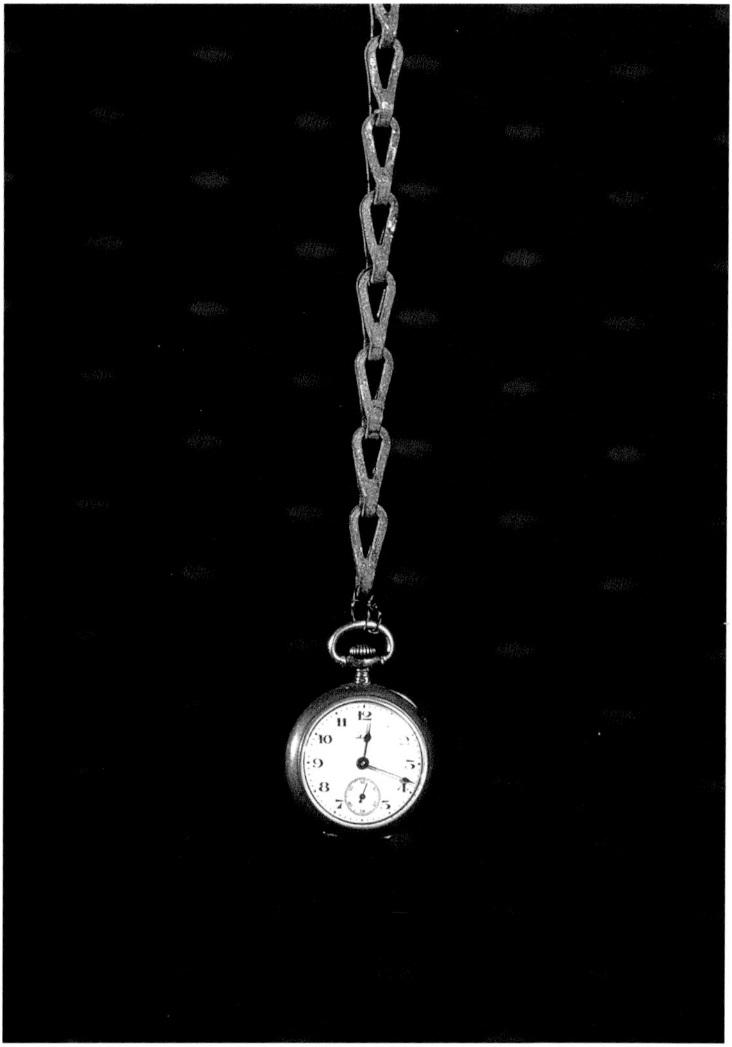

FIGURE 10 Louise Bourgeois, *Spider* (detail: grandfather's watch), 1997, steel and mixed media, 175 × 262 × 204 in. Courtesy Cheim & Read, New York. Photograph: Marcus Schneider

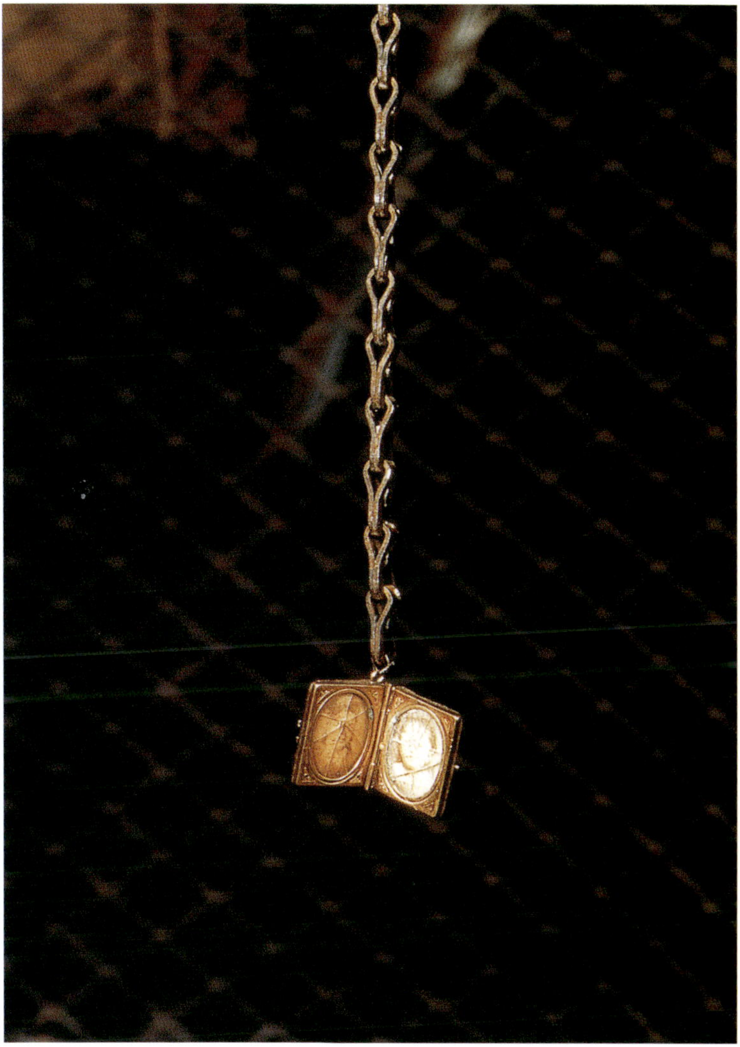

FIGURE 11 Louise Bourgeois, *Spider* (detail: tiny locket), 1997, steel and mixed media, 175 × 262 × 204 in. Courtesy Cheim & Read, New York. Photograph: Marcus Schneider

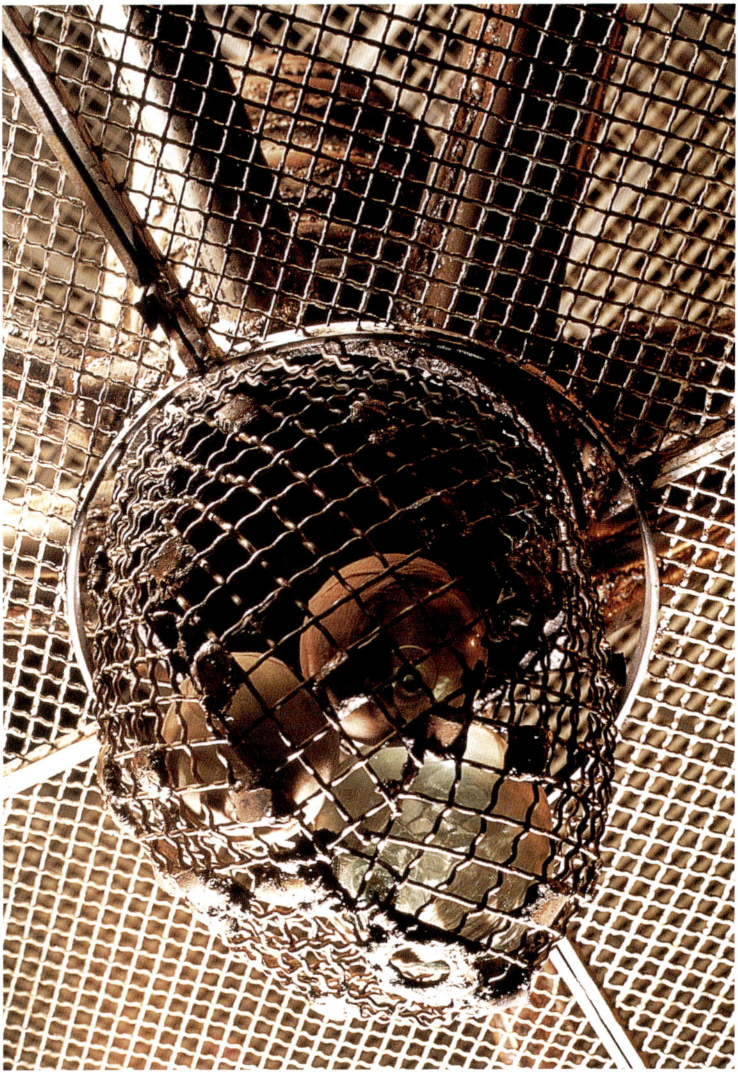

FIGURE 12 Louise Bourgeois, *Spider* (detail: eggs in a basket), 1997, steel and mixed media, 175 × 262 × 204 in. Courtesy Cheim & Read, New York. Photograph: Marcus Schneider

viewer standing outside as it is for the imaginary subject sitting in the chair, or for the lucky visitor allowed to enter and turn this virtual seat into an actual one. With this subject I must identify or I won't be able to see the eggs. Heteropathic identification is required to see them. From that position—which, in secured exhibition spaces, almost no viewer can reach, but all can imagine—the spider's legs converge to form a constellation (fig. 13).

The basket contains shiny, glass eggs, partly covered with nylon tights that look like thin rusted steel. The body of the spider opens to drop the eggs into the basket, which is thus transformed from part of her body into outside container. Where is the body's unity? The body is now vertical. Walking out backwards, I hit a leg. The alarm might sound. Get out of here now! Or you never will.

Description, as many specialists of narrative have pointed out, is challenged, dominated, if not ruined by narrative, whose handmaiden it is. Ever since Homer insisted that Achilles' shield could only be described as it was being made in Vulcan's foundry, description for its own sake has been an embarrassment to narrative. And even when description was foregrounded as the sole purpose of writing, its bond with the subject that is speaking about, perceiving, or acting upon the described object has been more rather than less insistently *narrated.* It is due to the participation of the viewing subject that any description, therefore, melts into the narration of the process that makes it possible.[3] But precisely how does narrative intervene in my attempt to describe *Spider?*

The first answer is simple and short. The account can only be an account of viewing the work. This is not, or not only, due to

3. On the theoretical point, see, for example, Gérard Genette's "Frontiers of Narrative." Svetlana Alpers' seminal study *The Art of Describing,* while based on an opposition between (Dutch) descriptive and (Italian) narrative art, does not provide a definition of description; nor does the author discuss the difficulty of separating the two modes.

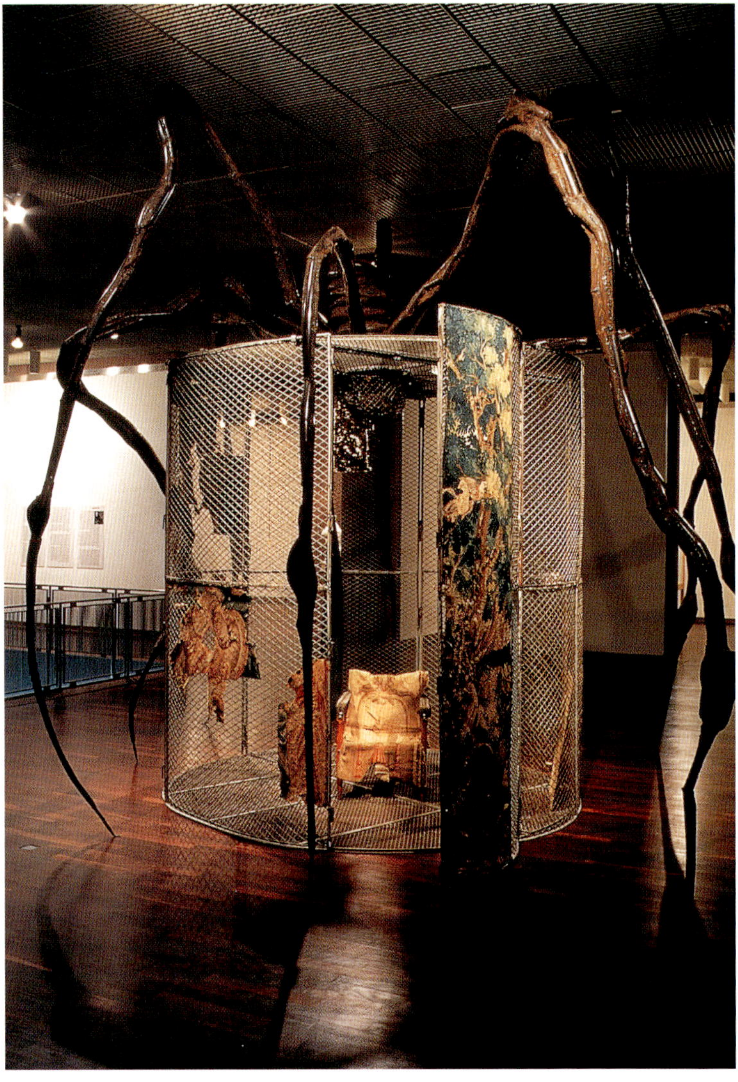

FIGURE 13 Louise Bourgeois, *Spider*, 1997, steel and mixed media, 175 × 262 × 204 in. Courtesy Cheim & Read, New York. Photograph: Marcus Schneider

the undeniable fact that viewing is by definition a process. Ever since Marcel Duchamp's *Optical Machines* from the 1920s, we have known that the rapid glance is a myth, or at least a mistake.[4] This work, instead, foregrounds, in many ways, represents, that obvious fact—obvious but massively repressed in the discourse on art. As is true of all works of visual art but clearly not obviously enough, here the viewer simply cannot see the entire work in one *Augenblick*. Many aspects of the work enforce a viewing that *takes time*, imposing an awareness of that temporality. And when culturally processed, time carries narrative.

The narrative of viewing rivals the narrative of memory, whose presence one senses but cannot grasp. For the memories here are not narrated; they are just put there, like the found objects that they, in fact, are. Memories are found objects that we routinely integrate into narrative frames derived from the cultural stock available to us. Unless, that is, they resist such integration because the place where they are found—the past of the recalling person—does not provide such ground for integration. This would be the case with events so horrific that the one to whom they happen lacks the necessary framework to experience them. This is what characterizes trauma.[5] By presenting memories as found objects, Bourgeois makes them appear as scraps or bits of a past that hover over the undecidable yet profound divide between memory and trauma, between narrative and compulsive reenactment in the dramatic mode. Through the need to experience the temporality of looking, the narratives that turn this particular *Cell* into a house also slam the door on the viewer trying to read the stories.

4. This insight has not prevented the space/time opposition between image and word to continue to flourish. On Duchamp's *Optical Machines*, see Krauss 1993. On Duchamp's aesthetic "attitude," see Thierry de Duve 1996.

5. For an elaboration of trauma, see Ernst van Alphen 1997.

Her stories of the past stick to our stories of looking, but they remain opaque. This is an important moment: the theoretical object declares war on narrative. But this war is waged by means of seduction. Thus, another dichotomy is questioned when "war" is fought with a self-reflective wink at such military metaphors and the semantics they reinforce.

Old bits of narrative stick to the cage's wall. The very surfaces that constitute it—the fragments of tapestry—also constitute visual barriers that make peeking into the cage an effort, steps taken one by one. The spider that names and claims this work also enforces an approach that precludes simultaneous viewing of its body and the *Cell* it hides, protects, and *is.* The tapestries are the walls they also decorate. It is precisely in this double function that they become indexes of architecture.

Enforcing a narrative awareness of the hiccuping temporality of viewing, the work destroys its own narrativity at the same time. Its overall shape already does that. The round form deploys time since you have to walk around it, yet prevents any attempt at gauging the length of that time span. Roundness offers no beginning, no end. And, once you have walked around the cage, avoiding collision with the hard bronze legs of the spider, the chair with its fragment of tapestry is still sitting there, mute and full of narrative, of tales broached but not revealed by the fragments encountered on my round.

More persistently perhaps, more obviously at any rate, the narratives whispered by the fragments of tapestry intervene, teasing my account, daring it to claim description and objectivity by means of irresistible tales from the past that threaten to take over, in the "third-person" voice, where the tales preexist my reading of them. Here, tales of renaissance or re-presented renaissance, always-already citations of and from ancient times, stop the walk around the cage, holding the viewer back with their beckoning once-upon-a-time-ness, like tar sticking to shoes. *Fabulas* of walkers and women, details of nature and ancient architectural settings capturing the acts of decorating in a temporality whose multiple layers can no longer be disentangled, stop that feminine figure about to insert fabric into a ring, suspending her movement. They also stop me. Trying to understand what is going on, I already participate in the restoration of the ancient narrative of decoration—a restoration that, in the present, is an act of building. Narrativity can no longer be disentangled from architecture. Without the former, the latter would fall apart. Without the latter, the former would have nowhere to go.

Most decisively, the attempt to describe flounders in the entanglement between object and process that this work, in the present of viewing, seems to utter. In the very act of describing, I am compelled to tell the story of what happens to me as I try. The object does not remain still. The relation it imposes on my eye, no, on my entire body—since I have to walk in order to see and avoid (the spider's legs) in order to approach (the cage)—is of a particular temporal kind, for that relation is subject to a movement in the time of now, a *Jetztzeit* according to Walter Benjamin, in which the sculpture tells itself through me. My bodily participation in this now-act tears and claws at the category of sculpture. With each step, this *Cell* gains momentum as a building.

Here, the distinction between narrative and description flounders; narrative emerges victorious and must be reckoned with. Rock hard, like a cliff beneath the seas, narrative remains. Its persistence and predominance, then, are not the problem, for why consider an inevitability problematic? Its modes, the ways it insinuates itself into what I set out to perform against it—visual description—militate against the illusion of visual purity that underlies the medium-essentialism inherited from modernism. This is a first way that *Spider* positions itself, Bourgeois' art, and contemporary visual experience within the messy realm of existence that admits no boundaries, either of space or time. Thus, *Spider* becomes the habitat of the present. This is the first theoretical contention that the work—in my reading of it—proposes. From the vantage point of art criticism, I find it essential to heed this assertion. Narrative, in this now-time, has a corollary in art criticism, a discourse that might do well to endorse this work's discursive revisionism, its theoretical thrust as a critique of narrative's predominance in the discourse of and on art. But this is a critique that shuns facile rejection as much as it turns its back on slavish, unreflected obedience to that cultural mode's tyranny.

THREE

Narrative and Its Discontents

[Life is] when it goes on "doing something," moving, exchanging material with its environment, and so forth, and that for a much longer period than we would expect an inanimate piece of matter to "keep going" under similar circumstances. ERWIN SCHROEDINGER[1]

A number of different deployments of narrative predominate in talk about art. All of these are both solicited and questioned by Bourgeois' work in general, and by *Spider* in particular. But the latter work does not stop at questioning the deployments. It offers a revision of each, proposing new ways of thinking this age-old mode of communicating through stories, so that, in the end, narrative can come forward again but in a new guise. What distinguishes the old narrative from the one *Spider* articulates and activates is temporality. By the imposition and foregrounding of the messy temporality involving *Jetztzeit,* Bourgeois' narrativity binds sculpture to architecture. But narrative as cement is no longer what it used to be.

The most common narrative modes can be characterized by their positioning as *anterior* stories. In the sharpest

1. This was Schroedinger's answer to the question put to him in 1944 while he was in exile from Germany: "What is the characteristic feature of life? When is a piece of matter said to be alive?"; cited by Evelyn Fox Keller (1995: 66–67). In the same paragraph, Keller refers to Schroedinger as "the father of quantum mechanics."

formulation, a visual work is thus considered an *illustration* of the narrative that precedes it and to which it is subordinated, its success being measured in terms of the degree to which it matches the story. Under the heading of anteriority, I wish to confront a variety of approaches at the same time, although the proponents of these approaches will tend to consider them fundamentally different. But *Spider* challenges them all under the same heading—under the roof of the spider's eggs.

Various practices of iconography exemplify the problems this narrative mode of anteriority poses. For example, iconographic analysis is often a search for antecedent works of art, other images in which motifs, poses, compositional schemata, conceptualizations, or allegories were already used, so that the later work is affiliated with visual predecessors. In other cases, iconographical analysis explains pictorial elements with reference to textual sources. Representations of mythical stories are referred back, for example, to Ovid's *Metamorphoses.* I know of no writing on Bernini's *Apollo and Daphne* (1622–25, Villa Borghese, Rome), for example, that does not "explain" or "describe" the sculpture in terms of Ovid's story.[2] Specific inflections and details are explained as visual interpretations of textual features of the story. Or, to give another example, Caravaggio's paintings are explained with reference to Counter-Reformation dogma and the discussion of fine points thereof.[3] Whether iconography seeks to pinpoint the antecedent story as the source of a perfect match or a significant deviation, or whether it construes the antecedent as a sounding board against which the posterior visual work can stand out in its difference, the narrative of anteriority uses the prior text or image as a measuring

2. For an example of this, but also, for extensive visuals, see the detailed study edited by Kristina Herrmann Fiore (1997).
3. See, for example, Pamela Askew's study *Caravaggio's "Death of the Virgin."*

stick. This is what iconography does to Bourgeois' work: the spiders are metaphors for the artist's mother; the tapestries come from, hence, are metonymies of, the parents' workshop. Why, then, can we not "own" those stories, read them off the page so that they replace the mute objects we see?

Regardless of whether this corresponds with the avowed wish of the writer, the major thrust of such anteriority narratives consists of diminishing the studied work's "originality," in a justified impulse to shed romantic notions of art. Thus, where Caravaggio or Rembrandt were once considered geniuses, they now have become craftsmen doing a job for patrons who, it must therefore be deduced, really "invented" the work.[4] Artists have cannily led the way to this much-needed revision of romantic preconceptions of art. And a work that integrates discarded perfume bottles, pieces of bone, and old fabric, a work where nothing in itself bears the artist's signature as "hand," must certainly agree with such a rejection of the idolatry of originality. It has, in fact, proposed that very rejection.

However welcome this antiromantic attitude may have been at the time, though, it has now become a paradoxical tool to undermine the very art it is alleged to serve,[5] for it defeats the point of visual art, which is not to reiterate but to innovate, to offer experiences and insights, sights and sites that we did not as yet possess. This has nothing to do with romantic originality but a lot to do with art's efficacy (rather than "essence"), with an understanding of art as process, with cultural life at the crossroads of significant events. Thus, by specifically ignoring the visuality of the particular work, a narrative of anteriority bypasses what the work

4. A striking example, up to its subtitle "genius under commission," is Bert Treffers' study of a few paintings by Caravaggio (1991).
5. For this argument, see my book *Quoting Caravaggio.*

of art as a theoretical object has to say. Objecting to this, I contend, is one of *Spider*'s theoretical propositions. It effectuates that proposition—"enunciates" it—through its imposition of a bodily participation by the viewer, who, caught up between narrativity and sculpturality, "builds" a home for old stories in the *now.*

Anteriority is also the backdrop of historicizing accounts that avoid iconography while remaining committed to a view of the history of art as an ongoing probing of issues of form. The anteriority, here, is entangled with the notion that each artist cannot but be embedded in, or "framed" by, the art of his or her time. This, of course, is true. But not all artists work within a single time. Bourgeois' work would obviously resist definition in terms of such periodizing gestures. Yet even a sophisticated critic such as Krauss lapses into this anteriority when she claims: "But Louise Bourgeois is an artist of the immediate postwar period—of the late 1940s and the 1950s—*not of the generation of the seventies*" (1999: 54; emphasis added). Against such relegation to the past, the messiness of *Spider*'s temporality is Bourgeois' mighty means of asserting it as firmly belonging to the *Jetztzeit,* to the now that her work, at this very moment and with your help, is building. Precisely because Krauss' analysis is among the best made of Bourgeois' work, its argument may be instructive.

To be fair, the context in which Krauss proffered this statement makes sense: an interpretation of *Fillette,* from 1968, or rather, of Mapplethorpe's 1982 photograph of Bourgeois with *Fillette,* which already complicated the periodization. But 1968 is not the immediate postwar period. Indeed, it was the year of the most radical break with that period, a break concerned, precisely, with the destructive effect of a reliance on anteriority that lacked engagement with the present. Both that significant year and Bourgeois' almost performance-art-like work on and in the present makes the periodization in Krauss' remark not quite adequate. And yet, the subsequent argument that Bourgeois' work—not only *Fillette*—is best considered through Brancusi's reduction of form, posits the anteriority narrative clearly and emphatically as a frame within which to articulate the specific effects of the art. Unlike most, Krauss does not superpose this narrative with obedience to influence but instead argues for Bourgeois' polemic with her predecessors. Krauss' inevitable subtext is a binary opposition: this rather than that; Brancusi rather than later "scandal" art.

As a result of this subtext, Krauss ends up with a double argument. On the one hand, Bourgeois is distinctive in her deployment of what the critic calls *part-objects,* a Lacan-informed view of the relation to the object of desire, rather than a (formal) identification with fragmentation of self. This is a highly relevant interpretation. On the other hand, this specificity is referred back to "the surrealist background from which it springs" (68). Here, anteriority becomes a prison. The fixation on chronology that anteriority narratives espouse makes it impossible to endorse a logic that would allow Bourgeois to prefigure rather than to follow.

Anteriority is also the ground against which biographical or psychoanalytical accounts of art place the work. Here, the timeline spans not the history of mythology and art but the life of the artist. This life as a narrative allegedly inhabits the work it yields, shaping it and informing its affective and aesthetic power. And when biographical criticism explains motifs with reference to the artist's life, biographism blends with iconography. This happens, for example, when Bourgeois' use of tapestry fragments is explained through the biographical fact of her parent's having worked in tapestry restoration rather than by focusing on the possible meanings and effects of—to mention one of the most obvious features of this recycling of fragments—the *fragmentation* of old fabrics.

Don't misunderstand me; I, too, find Bourgeois' background important. I imagine the young girl busy in a workshop whose smell alone must have infused her body with all the moods that historicity and times past produce in one growing up and dreaming. I imagine Emma Bovary's dreams killing her as an after-effect of growing up. But Bourgeois did not drown there. She grew up and out of that workshop, and what she does with the fragments of that past, in a precise sense, is to *build* the walls that stand between her and old times, in the habitat of now-time. As an antidote to the smell of dust, the young girl's perfume bottles are refreshing. The leap from a sense of pastness to Bourgeois' biography remains subject to scrutiny. As Anne M. Wagner put it: "I still want to know what biography and autobiography compensate *for*." She continues with a suggestion for interpretation of this critical habit when she writes: "I think it is right to locate that anxiety or absence as bound up in certain other narratives—these concerning sculpture and representation—with which Bourgeois' work has been declared to be at odds" (1999: 6). In this interpretation, it appears, then, that one kind of anteriority narrative—the biographical one—is called upon to redeem another otherwise hopeless kind that is, in a sense, biography's other, namely, "proper" art history, the history of media and forms.

Within biographism, other blending occurs too—although it should be impossible. I am referring here to the appeal to the artist's intentions, to her own interpretations of her works and her own explanations of how they happened, as it combines with the psychoanalytical slant of criticism. This is contradictory. For biographical and psychoanalytical narrative models of explanation utilize a different, if not radically opposed, conception of subjectivity and agency. Biographical criticism is grounded in a rationalist, unified conception of subjectivity as effectively intentional. It appeals to the artist's intention. And in cases such as Bourgeois', where the artist is extremely articulate and strongly committed to preventing the misunderstandings that constantly threaten her complex work so as to present her work according to her intentions, the criticism of the work tends to reiterate simply what the artist says it means. The result is the frequent quotation of things she has written or said with presentations of her work. This biographism is blended with iconography when critics reiterate, after Bourgeois, that the figure of the spider is a metaphor for her mother's protective and caring attitude within family life.

But if we want to dream about a nonreductive engagement with visual art, this reason-based subjectivity must be allowed to go to sleep. In its dreams, then, it will encounter its counterpart, for psychoanalytical criticism is by definition committed to exploring unconscious impulses alleged to pour forth from the work. Strictly speaking, such criticism cannot appeal to intentionalist statements at all. The conception of the subject underlying such criticism is, or ought to be, that of a split subject, who, to use Freud's words, is not master in his or her own house.

In the case of Bourgeois' *Cells,* and particularly *Spider,* this Freudian phrase is strikingly apt, for these works appear in shape as well as content to be houses in just such a double sense. The *Cells* are, or represent, houses in a literal sense, in the enclosed shape and shelter they suggest. This is their primal sense of architecture.[6] They are both building blocks and complete houses, body-houses. In this sense, they recall Bourgeois' earlier series

6. "Primal" as in Freud's concept of the primal scene, which occurs when the child witnesses parental intercourse and fails to understand it. This primal visual experience is formative and can be traumatic. Within the short duration of the experience of a *Cell,* the subliminal sense of *house* is just such a formative experience that is strong in its impact even if the precise nature of that impact cannot be pinned down. See, for a definition of *primal scene,* Laplanche and Pontalis 1973.

called *Femme-Maison,* through which Bourgeois' work moved pivotally from two- to three-dimensional. Here, the *Cells* militate against the predominant model in that art of building the house as a unified, idealized, symmetrical body. And they are, represent, or rather, *perform* the house where the Freudian subject whose own house it is, is not master.

There are two reasons for this, according to Bourgeois' *Spider* in its persona as theoretical object. First, figuratively, the *Cells* are houses of the mind, sheltering and facilitating the childhood memories they obviously house. The huge spider brings in its wake the small child who first saw it. That anteriority, instead of the biographical one, infuses the work with an outrageous instability of scale that turns a sculpture into a building and back again. This is the level where narrativity—not specifically narrative content—serves as the cement that builds the house. Second, as Briony Fer points out, the particular "theory" of conceitedness that speaks through Bourgeois' installation sculptures—and which I here analyze for *Spider*—requires a "house," a habitat for the subject to be, precisely, *not* master of.[7] Instead, "conceitedness" functions on the dual level of the relationship between subject and other, in a one-to-one connection, and *simultaneously* on the level of the relationship between the subject—the one—and her surroundings—many, embodied by the house. The walls are, then, permeable, a truly Derridean *frame* that delimits and protects, as well as opens up to the outside world: the surroundings. In this duality, the subject cannot, by definition, be master.

The Freudian sensibility rather than the content of the *Cells* as houses of the mind consists, moreover, of a precise, sensitive, very subtle resonance with the famous master/house metaphor from

7. See Fer 1999: 40–41.

the creator of psychoanalysis. For, masterful works of art that they are, "mastery" is not the sense they convey. Instead, "mystery" is more like it. Their strong affect and power of meaning-production suggest precisely the kind of subjectivity that would generate what cultural philosopher Walter Benjamin phrased as "ungrasped symbolism" and what psychoanalyst Christopher Bollas termed "the unthought known." Something the subject senses and upon which it acts but which it cannot articulate in a fully rational discourse—the intellectual discourse of artist's statements, for example. If the subject could just *say* it, what would be the point of making art, of saying it through art? Yet at the same time, this "unthought known" *is* something the subject knows, and needs to make and mold, so that it can actively—but outside of intellectual discourse—participate in the cultural process that leads to knowledge.[8]

Boldly, then, Bourgeois' *Spider* engages a theoretical debate with Freud, shifting this master's tendency to anteriority narratives back to where, according to *The Interpretation of Dreams,* they emerge: in the visual present.[9] This "debate" with psychoanalysis, rather than a subjection of her work to it, turns the metaphor of the mind's house, whose master does not master it, into a literal, embodied work of architecture. The "arch-" of the past is provided with the roof (*tect*) that leaks mother (through the eggs) and whose key dangles uselessly inside.

8. Both of these authors use their respective concepts to develop a notion of "visual thought" as a richer, thicker substitute for narrative. On Walter Benjamin's development of his concept of thought-images and the ungrasped symbolism, see Weigel 1996, esp. 80–83. Bollas' account (1987) of the multiply-split subjectivity in dreams is eminently apt to help rethink psychoanalytical criticism of visual art. See also my article "Dreaming Art."
9. Freud's work on visual art (in)famously falls short of the visual impact of his theory. See, for example, his essay on Leonardo. The argument I am making here is at the core of Damisch's essay on Piero della Francesca (1997).

The strong sense of mood, memory, and mystery that all the *Cells* emanate, partakes of this realm of the unthought known. Accounting for the *Cells* through the words of the artist (alone), then, would do them a profound injustice. If Bourgeois is such a strong spokeswoman for her own work, it is because *thought,* reason, is so very important to her art. The *Cells* are the work of Descartes' daughter,[10] who grudgingly takes up Vitruvius' legacy in a revisionist conception of architecture that does not allow reduction to reason. But on the woman of one *Femme-Maison* stands a house (fig. 14); or, in other cases, on the top of a woman's body stands a house (fig. 15). If she makes works that are so replete with childhood memories into such fragmented, allusive, yet powerfully present narratives, it is because she is also Freud's friend. She knows, even if many of her critics don't, that listening to her is fine but repeating her words (only) reduces her work to just one side of a multifarious, multilayered complexity.

Biographical and psychoanalytical narrative forms of criticism are different in principle yet similar in their deployment of anteriority. In the biographical form, the artist's statements are a welcome source of information, from which the story preceding the work is then constructed—or, as the claim goes, *re*constructed. In the psychoanalytical forms, the search is not for statements but for facts, even if the factfinder will often need to "forget" the taboo on overly explicit, hence, conscious, pronouncements by the artist.[11]

But the similarity is even more devastating when we consider the mode of reasoning that underlies the anteriority in each. As has been argued often enough, the relation between facts and

10. See Meyer-Thoss 1992: 68–75.

11. See my discussion of the problem of intentional criticism, specifically in relation to narrative, in chap. 7 of my book *Travelling Concepts* (in press).

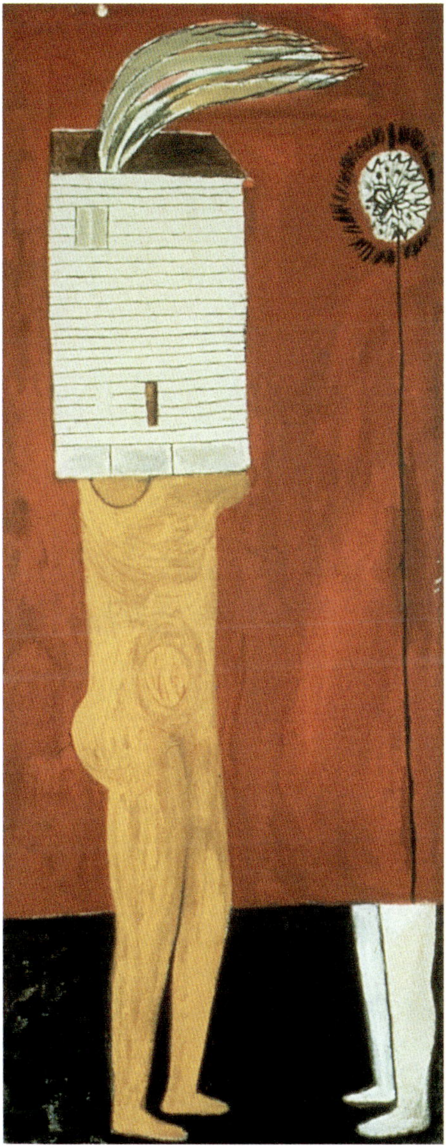

FIGURE 14
Louise Bourgeois, *Fallen Woman (Femme-Maison),* 1946–47, oil on linen, 36 × 14 in. Collection John D. Kahlbetzer. Photograph: Donald Greenhaus

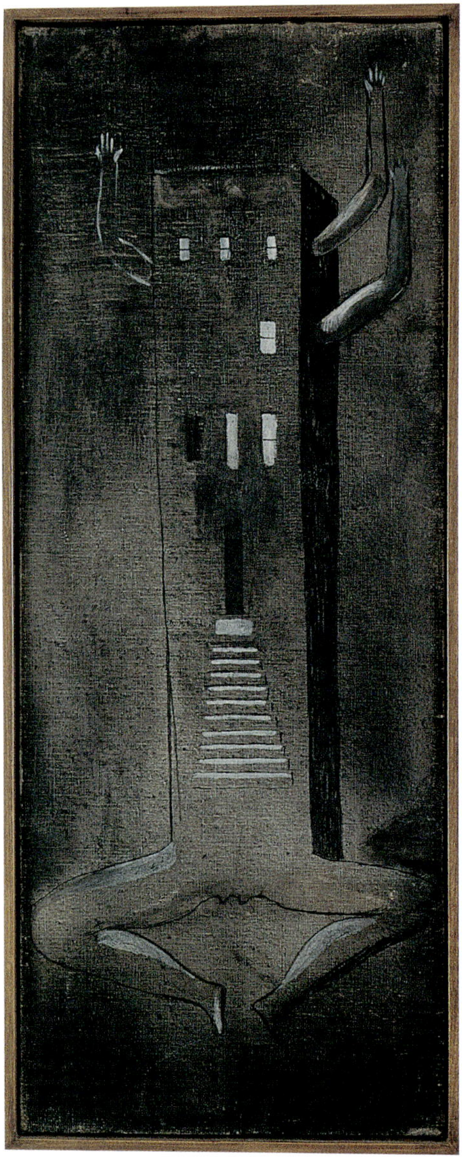

FIGURE 15
Louise Bourgeois, *Femme-Maison,* ca. 1946–47, oil on linen, 36 × 14 in. Collection John D. Kahlbetzer. Photograph: Donald Greenhaus

works can only be alleged if it is unavowedly based on a deterministic fallacy that fails to account for the logic of framing inherent in such reasonings. Hence, even in terms of explicit, rational logic, anteriority narratives fail to account for the work.[12]

As a consequence, in any deployment of narrative based on such forms of anteriority, one can only face contradiction. To anticipate my conclusion concerning the meaning and impact of *Spider* as theoretical object, I submit that Bourgeois' work embodies that contradiction, indicts, then traverses it, to move beyond it and propose a different kind of narrativity. Iconographically speaking, her work is non- or even antifigurative. At the same time, it is far from abstract. Wildly figurative in fact, it nevertheless precludes an analysis that relies on figuration. It is as bodily as it is, and as such it is unreadable. In this sense, it militates against an iconographic "reading-off-the-page" or translation according to a dictionary-based mode of reading.[13]

True, the spider hovering over the cage in *Spider* is indeed a spider, a representation of one. In combination with its realistic shape, its hyperbolic size insists on that. But here the trouble begins, for this hyperbole makes it unreadable again. How do we get beyond tautology? First, this spider is a spider. It thus marks the futility of figurative, realistic reading. Second, the spider's size recalls Freud's witty remark on the unreadability of widely printed letters on a map. This remark was taken up by Lacan—but prophetically by Edgar Allan Poe before him—in his analysis of an overzealous prefect of the Paris police. That good fellow was unable to find a compromising letter because it was *not* hidden but

12. On the flawed logic of anteriority-based "contextualism," e.g., see Norman Bryson 1994, which draws on Jonathan Culler's justly famous author's preface to his book *Framing the Sign*.
13. The major impact of Krauss' proposal to read Bourgeois' work in terms of part-object is to suspend the opposition between abstract and figurative. See esp. 1999: 54–55.

displayed before his nose, pulling on his nose, as it were.[14] *Spider* makes the case for such blindness due to scale, integrating a Freudian with a scientific argument that goes back to Leibnizian mathematics.[15]

But this integration is itself a good case for the kind of topological reasoning that fills this scientific engagement with baroque thought. It is on this level that *Spider* challenges the use of anteriority narrative as flawed reasoning. For topology destroys linearity by making embedding, not sequence, a principle of narrative time: embedding—an enfolding of one thing within another, a body within a house. Each element of *Spider* comprises both itself and the whole of which it is a part. This is not simply a move away from narrative to architecture, but the invention of an architecture that encompasses the very material out of which it also consists: sculpture, bodiliness, narrative. As a result of subjecting the spider and its cell (and its viewer) to a revision of scale that precludes visibility *and* to a figuration of repression (a theorizing, not an acting out of it), what emerges is, precisely, a spider that makes the point that anteriority narratives inhere in it yet remain out of reach. Thus Bourgeois the artist "explains" why the statements of Bourgeois the person, serious and to-the-point as they are, cannot, must not, stand in for a critical engagement with her work. They are just additional narratives that change as they travel through time.

This third point involves another move away from the representational bias that the spider first solicited, paradoxically *figured,*

14. Lacan's analysis triggered an impassioned debate, now available in a volume edited by Muller and Richardson (1988). See Anne Lowenthal 1996 and esp. Hanneke Grootenboer's superb discussion of *trompe l'oeil* painting (1999) on this issue of excessive visibility turning into invisibility.
15. See Deleuze's discussion of Leibniz's ideas on perception (1993), and also Serres on Leibnizian mathematics (1968). For the relevance of baroque mathematics—and especially baroque scale—for contemporary art, see my *Quoting Caravaggio.*

or configured, in the spider's position in *Spider.* To put it simply, the huge spider cannot be isolated from the round cell of woven steel. The basket filled with eggs is both her body and her yield. She is not just hovering over the cage, but once we look from inside the cage—which we should do but most often cannot—the ceiling is and is not the spider's body, the part of it that lays eggs, that projects a future beyond anteriority.

Countering as they do the translation of elements into words, works like the *Cells,* with their dense self-enclosure and complexly structured unity, insist on the failure of element-by-element translation for rendering or explaining the work as a whole. Elements that solicit biographical commentary—such as the spider, whose obsessive presence compels viewers to wonder what it means—become particularly troublesome for such translation when they loom over a richly inhabited *Cell* of which they are an inherent part even if they do not constitute it entirely.

Moreover, the history of twentieth-century sculpture that Bourgeois' work is often said to encompass does not allow us to box this art into any one of its main currents.[16] Here, it is not the active antifigurative thrust performed through figuration but the active dialogic attitude of the work that precludes a narrative of art history in terms of "influence." Indeed, it is possible to analyze Bourgeois' work—and it has been done effectively—in relation to all successive phases of modern sculpture, from Rodin to Brancusi and Picasso, and from abstract expressionism to postmodernism.[17]

Rodin's unfinished surfaces, Brancusi's excessively polished ones, Picasso's refusal of perspective, abstract expressionism's insistence

16. As presented, for example, by Rosalind Krauss' now classic study *Passages in Modern Sculpture* (1977).

17. For an analysis of such relations to, for example, Rodin, Picasso, and Brancusi, see Crone and Graf Schaesberg 1998: 71–80.

on bypassing figuration in self-expression, postmodernism's refusal of the latter and its recycling, instead, of the exterior past in nonautographic modes: *Spider* speaks of them all. In the face of this work's formal and semantic engagement with all these predecessors, it comes as no surprise that the only way criticism manages to circumvent, or counter, the strong predominance of the biographical kind of anteriority narrative is by shifting from that kind to its formalist-historical counterpart, the narrative of what came before. But the point is, *Spider,* even less than some of the more evidently sculptural works, cannot be reduced to any one of these ideas. The seduction of anteriority in general—and of anteriority narratives in which "art" structured according to the family metaphor of successive generations constitutes the fabula whose self-evident autonomy cannot be questioned—is enormous when the work under discussion is so willfully polemically engaged. The relations between *Spider* and these predecessors can be pinpointed as meaningful. But it is harder to define what *kind* of relations they are. The narrative model of development is too tightly bound to oedipal structure to open up insight into the *actuality* that largely determines *Spider's* effect. For as soon as one takes a closer look at the nature of these relations, they turn out to be ambivalent. Far from being "influenced" by her visual and artistic environment, the artist "discusses" that environment, past or present; she doesn't step in for the ride but "explains" why she doesn't.

Such narratives are problematic even within the framework of the biographically inclined critical tradition. In the case of Bourgeois' late recognition, the question of canonicity poses itself.[18] Although Bourgeois' work has become canonical, its specific posi-

18. See Altieri 1984.

tion within the canon remains indeterminate. And if, thus phrased, the impossibility of assigning this artist a place in the canon appears to be deplorable, I would prefer to consider the way the art itself engages, criticizes, and leaves behind the major trends of twentieth-century sculpture as what most sharply defines her work. For, in this domain as well, the work not only undermines (art-historical) narratives of anteriority but also offers alternatives for them. Thus it rearticulates the notion of "influence" itself, its passivity, its grounding in anteriority that mortifies the later artist and locks him or her up in an oedipally tinted rivalry. *Spider* as theoretical object again speaks up to this tendency of anteriority narrative to promote oedipalism. More productive than the idea of influence allows, *Spider* lays the past's eggs.[19]

Moreover, attempts to position Bourgeois within the art of the century that her work is so frequently said to span lose their appeal as articulations of what defines her work as soon as one becomes aware of other art-historical relationships, such as, most notoriously, with the baroque.[20] In sculpture after Picasso and Brancusi, such connections break the timeline that informs the ideology of evolution. And, once the homogeneous timeline of development is broken by such relationships to older art, these relationships, too, become dialogic rather than one-sided and forward-pushing, as in "influence." It is precisely through Bourgeois' relationship to baroque sculpture that she offers a radically innovative exploration of sculptural narrativity—in dialogue with both modernism and the baroque. And the form of this explo-

19. Michael Baxandall (1985) made this argument long ago, in an effective deconstruction of the notion of "influence."

20. A marble sculpture from 1970 is explicitly titled *Baroque.* For a reproduction, see Crone and Graf Schaesberg 1998: 58. Another sculpture, from 1967, is titled *Homage to Bernini* (85). See Anne Wagner's incisive comment on this work in "Bourgeois Prehistory, or the Ransom of Fantasies" (1999: 12).

ration is architectural: in three dimensions, a topologically structured spatiality turned paradoxical by a flipping of scale, she builds a baroque chapel, but one in which the body is inside and outside at the same time. By the same token, this relationship itself, as a revision of the way we tend to look at art, rethinks historicism and its narrative compulsions.

In addition, then, to such dialogical engagements with past art, or through them, narrative in or with *Spider* shifts its focus from anteriority to the work's present, to its *Jetztzeit.* This more promising but also more complex strand of narrative reasoning concerns the relationship between sculpture and viewer or, more precisely, the act of viewing. If viewing is an act deployed in a process of interaction, then the account of that process takes a narrative form. For if narrative is an account deployed in time of a series of related events, which, in turn, occur in time, then the process the viewer stands before—or, where sculpture is concerned, walks around, being infused by the effects and affects it emanates—can only be reconstructed, analyzed, and criticized in a form that renders that movement through time.[21]

Spider both requires and "thematizes" this processual narrativity, as I will call it here. This narrativity is more than an alternative to the anteriority-based narrative modes. It provides those modes with critical commentary as well as with more "thickness," with another layer of narrative meaning that may resolve some of the conflicts that burden these modes. The sculptures, the *Cells,* and *Spider* specifically, tell a story of visual engagement which, although anchored in the past of the moment of viewing, proposes the act of viewing in the present as an active recall of this past. Thus, overruling anteriority, the *Cells* reactivate old stories in new moments.

21. One of the consequences of this point for the language of criticism is the need to involve the analytical idiom of narratology. See for this Bal 1997.

In this context, another related aspect of narrative that Bourgeois revitalizes in highly significant ways shifts narrative even more prominently into a different temporality. This aspect is grounded in the sense-based bodiliness of the specific present that each act of viewing produces and shapes. Here, in *Spider,* the substance of narrative is not so much the process of viewing as the work imagines and offers it in fictional form, but the actual "utterance" or "enunciation" that it performs in a temporality rigorously located in the present. Unlike the second narrative (the *processual* one staged by the artist), and unlike the first (the *anteriority* narrative imagined by the critic), this third, *performative* narrative is done by the viewer. It blurs the distinction between narrative as it is traditionally construed and drama in the Aristotelian sense of action. But it also revises the idea of narrative in such a way that it is able to specify narrative presenting, the making present through narrative, of a reality that is more than fictional.

Although fantasy-based and appealing to fantasy, this reality is offered as utterly important, indeed, vital, for our need to integrate into today's real world, which is so increasingly informed by what is called "virtual reality." We can aptly call the embodied, present reality "told" by *Spider* as "virtual" according to the broad but culturally important definition of virtuality as "fictions of presence."[22] Thus, rather than being overruled by a preestablished narrative that subordinates it to convention, *Spider* helps us to understand its own cultural contribution by helping us to understand aspects of narrative itself.

And this, I insist—and here is the point of the question of narrative—*Spider* does by foregrounding its most notorious visual aspects, in the way these embody the tenacious refusal of the di-

22. See Morse 1998: esp. 3–35.

chotomies that rule our culture. On all levels of visuality—and that is where the "unthought known" resides—Bourgeois' work categorically rejects those dichotomies: between mind and body, abstraction and figuration, visuality and tactility, flatness and volume, time and space. These fundamental dichotomies generate other more directly recognized dichotomies such as male-female and white-black, but also ones that tend to prevent visual art from achieving its effectivity as *thought:* oppositions that cast visual art as spatial, and narrative as temporal, confining each to a restricted domain of visual body and narrative mind, hence, semiotically, disabling both.[23] *Spider,* like many of Bourgeois' other works, integrates a strong and embodied visuality with a story-telling activity that does not allow one to take over the other. What holds all the poles together so they are no longer opposites but mates, is the architectural sense of *habitat* that shelters us while we contribute, in real time, to building it. The interplay of light and form is thickened with an interplay of time and space, played inside and out.

23. For a tenacious recurrence of these dichotomies in discussions of visual art, see Mitchell 1985.

FOUR

Refocusing Attention

> Images have been transformed from static representations of the world into spaces in which events happen that involve and engage people to various degrees in physical space. MARGARET MORSE[1]

Let us leave behind, then, the model of anteriority narrative, if only to estrange an ingrained cultural habit. I propose we shed that habit, in its biographical, psychoanalytical, and art-historical guises, respectively. Instead, in this chapter I will articulate, with, through, and for *Spider,* a different kind of narrativity that anteriority narrative would render all but invisible. To grasp that other narrativity, I will unpack the complex, multilayered ways that *Spider* invents, articulates, and conveys the embodied narrativity that glues together the building blocks of this body-house. Resisting the narrative layers that, in the guise of the tapestry fragments, literally impose narrative as a hindrance, I must, regretfully, ignore them for the moment. I regret this imposed neglect, for I, too, fall for narrativity. And through its tapestry fragments, *Spider* acknowledges this habit of mine, respects it, and gently prods its traps. For the fragments lure with narrative but also shield it. Just as the legs of the spider intimidate but

1. Morse 1998: 21.

must be passed because the fragments beckon with their strange stories, so the fragments lure but must be passed because the inside of the cell invites us in. For, inside the cage, *subject position* is proposed in the form of the chair, beckoning. This is another strand of the work's theoretical discourse. The chair *is,* or *stands for*—in the sense that semiotics defines the sign as standing for—subject position as a place for the subject to be and to interact from with his or her environment. *Spider,* by means of its chair, which is geographically its inner core, proposes subjectivity as position, defined by connectedness in the dual sense evoked in the previous chapter. It is a place, empty, ready for the taking, were it not for the fabric stiffly taking up the seat. From that enviable position I would be able to see the spider's eggs properly, to feel the protective reassurance—or is it frightening confinement? This I cannot know from the outside. Bourgeois would have let me in, but the museum's insurance company would not. From the chair I would be able to grasp the key, unlock the door of the past that tantalizingly remains remote. That chair is the place for me, on the stage, inside the house—and I can only look at it.

For the literal door I don't need that key hanging there, since it stands open. But I wouldn't dream of slipping inside, with that spider so huge standing guard, its body-basket already inside. Or would I? After a while, yes; the spider becomes friendly with time. But its guarding function is taken over by the institutional restrictions that even childhood memories cannot break. So, looking inside, peering in, is all I can do. Roundness is centripetal; it invites spiraling inward until the middle point is reached. But spider-guards, wired cages, and museum spaces recommend staying out. The body is severed from the eye. The door stands open, but not widely enough for a human body to slip through. Similarly, an art installation, surrounded by the art installation of which this *Cell* is both an element and a smaller version, holds off the touch as it invites the eye.

That eye sets out to wander around inside the cage. It sees things that could not be seen from a distance. Those small glass jars, those perfume bottles attract me like flickering charms. They are so pretty, yet ordinary enough. Collectors' items for teenage girls. Why are those glass jars, with their pharmaceutical, medical look, left to dry, upside down, on those metal stands? Why are those perfume bottles hanging on steel chains? They belong to memory, but I don't have access to the realm of the senses that builds memories through them. What are they, what do they do, so unrelated to either the chair—alias subject position—or the bones or tapestry? Inside the cage, they seem also isolated, wilfully; strung up so as to avoid contact with, contamination by, any surface that might induce decay. These small objects housed within the *Cell* spell out one of the meanings of "cell"—the one that is tied to small-scale existence, agglutination, and life.

The organicist model that cells propose as bodily atoms and principles of life yet also as threats to health is both represented by these bottles and countered by them. Small containers, they share the shape with those cells we cannot see but of which we see so many representations in the world of medicine, disease, biology—the most "vital" science of the present and the future. Miniature bottles, they are gigantic cells.[2]

These bottles achieve two different effects. They question scale and refocus attention. But didn't the gigantic and encompassing spider herself already question scale? This first challenge addresses the threat of monumental seduction that looms over the spider.

2. Within the *Cells* series, these bottles resonate with others, most notably *Precious Liquids* (1992), with its exuberance of glass bubbles, but also with *In and Out* (1995), with its mirroring balls, and in a different way, with *Cell II* (1991), where perfume bottles are neatly displayed on a mirroring tray.

Scale as such, not the choice between either huge or tiny, determines the inner sense of bodily scale that shakes up the viewer, accustomed as he is to be the measure of all things. The bottles also refocus attention, away from narrative as we know it. These two effects lead us to the architecturality, to the interplay of light and form.[3]

The bottles do their double work on the mode of still life. They are just objects; as far as they are concerned, the work is a still life not a story. From the vantage point of these tiniest participants in the installation, the work's order obeys paratactic not syntactic arrangement; juxtaposition, accumulation, even potential clutter; not one thing after another, nor all at once, but one thing, then another thing, then another, where "then" is not prescriptively fixed—a paradoxical *time*-consuming arrangement. No sequential narrative, no development, no life story. But the eye is compelled to travel even if it chooses its own itinerary, and thus time unfolds in the act of viewing; in viewing's present, *Jetztzeit.* The travel through the different rooms of a large, strange house.[4]

This traveling of the eye beckons me in. The journey from one glass bottle to another takes time. Seen myopically, each begins to look like a complete body, with shoulders and a head, the edge of the stopper like hair recently bobbed by a hairdresser with thirties tastes, the bottom like feet dancing; the bottle as a whole, a Charleston dress. From object to object, then, the eye walks, roaming from room to room on a tour that takes time but whose sequence remains free. A narrative of architectural tourism or rather, a visit to the unknown house inhabited by a friend. Had I

3. See O'Toole 1995: 134.

4. The work these bottles do is a kind of underside or subcoding of representation, comparable to Jana Sterbak's *Condensed* or Roni Horn's *Asphere,* both sculptures that become performative through their enforcement of a different kind of attention. On Sterbak's work in relation to refocusing attention, see Nemiroff 1991; on Horn's *Asphere,* see Gorovoy 1998/99.

been inside, as the artist would like people to be, the objects would have been closer, but the trip would have taken the same amount of time.

The round form of this *Cell* now seems just a first, encompassing notice of the refusal of linearity, of the sequential order that narrative as we know it requires. Doesn't the *Spider* here, precisely, *surround* the cell it also constitutes? The bottles are tiny versions of the work as a whole. They are also miniatures of the eggs at its center. Scale loses its stability.[5] Hovering between tiny and gigantic, the work rearticulates Blaise Pascal's baroque image of the universe in terms of the infinitely small and the infinitely great.

Challenging the certainties that viewers bring to this *Cell*, measuring scale in relation to their own body, the effect of this work on scale is dizzying. For, once I peer through the woven steel of the cage, once I stop to look inside and scrutinize these nostalgic bottles, the usual relationships between time, space, and body become mixed up. I enter within the spider's body yet remain locked outside the cage. The chair has a normal size, ready to receive the body of subjects such as me, but the bottles, although as normal in size as perfume bottles, are so small they enforce a myopic look that makes the chair appear, in the corner of my eye, too large, intimidating like a royal throne. Distance hampers sight yet proximity imposes itself, bestowing elephantine proportions on the viewing subject. Looking through the openings in the steel fabric, I cannot see the bottles that attract my eye and the iron grid that keeps my body out, simultaneously. So I suspend the grid and virtually go inside.

Here, I submit, *Spider*'s narrativity resides. And in its status as theoretical object, *Spider* proposes this particular kind of narrativ-

5. See Susan Stewart's very relevant study, whose title now seems to sum up a program similar to *Spider*'s: *On Longing: Narratives of the Miniature, the Gigantic, the Souvenir, the Collection.*

ity as an allegory on which a different kind of art-writing is invited to model itself. The physical instability thus generated prepares us for *the still life coming to life.* Myopically fixated on these mute things, solitude shuts me up in a place that excludes me. As Norman Bryson has presented it, the genre of still life is defined in the first place by the absence of the human figure.[6] This absence, then, enters center stage. It has always been there, in the shape of that empty chair, whose layer of tapestry, I now realize, hyperbolically mocks emptiness, offering a body-shaped *trompe l'oeil* wall panel ending in a hanging tassel. A wall of a room as a seat: Where can the subject dwell? But now that I am gazing at these mute and empty things, my own mind-and-body becomes the stage of that emptiness. Psychoanalysis has long ago defined desire in terms of lack. But desire is a form of narrative, setting in motion a movement outward, an engagement with the other.

This is one example of Bourgeois' work on narrative through the act of building or architecture. Simultaneously subverting and soliciting both the narrative of desire's movement outward and the narrative that psychoanalysis constructs out of that process, the movement here goes inward, not outward. This movement cannot go anywhere, ending as it does in the aporia of a literal non sequitur: an empty little bottle, a container containing emptiness, placed somewhere, inside but not in the center, in an order that is as necessary to as it is outside of narrative logic.

"Still-life is the world minus its narratives, or, better, the world minus its capacity for generating narrative interest," writes Bryson (1989: 60). Interpreting Juan Sánchez Cotán's (1561–1627) still-life paintings, which the artist himself called *bodegones,* Bryson sees in these extremely frugal ("anorexic," meaning "without desire") rep-

6. See Bryson 1989.

resentations of humble vegetables disposed according to a mathematically calculated geometry of *hyperbola,* a lesson in unlearning narrative interest. To narrate, he says, "is to name what is unique: the singular actions of individual persons" (60). Such narrativity is the equivalent of monumentality. As I will argue later, it is the aspect of modernist architecture as Comas described it—"a debate between walls and columns, axiality and the dispersion of focal points, centrality of interest or its displacement to the periphery, frontal presentation and an oblique or circular route" (1998: 7)—that *Spider* "debates" and, after serious consideration, rejects. Still life trains the eye to unlearn the trap of such narrative.

In the Catholic seventeenth century, such exercises belonged to the cultivation of Loyolan spirituality.[7] These exercises rested on the paradoxical use of the senses to concentrate on spirituality, and on the elimination of narrative—in Bryson's sense—in favor of a narrative of concentration. But the display of ordinary yet nostalgia-inducing perfume bottles in *Spider,* tokens of a worldly femininity, can hardly be construed in religious terms.

Yet these bottles are and do precisely what Cotán's still-life paintings do, albeit for a different world and a different time. They engage the senses in a bare narrative of bodiliness. Like Cotán's paintings, the arrangement of the bottles is extremely calculated for balance yet not narratively motivated. Like the cabbage, quince, or leek in Cotán's bare, gray larders, they are the opposite of unique. Like those elements of creation, they are contingent, empty of meaning, tokens of endlessly repeatable production, of an infinite series—importantly, though, man-made. No individual is attached to them: not in their being, not in their production, not in their use, which they, temporarily, do not have; from which they are, literally, suspended.

7. Ibid.; see also, in a theological and literary perspective, Pranger 1997, on Loyola's spiritual exercises.

Bryson calls the depiction of such utter ordinariness *rhopography,* the depiction of "those things which lack importance, the unassuming material base of life that 'importance' constantly overlooks" (61). This humiliation of attention offers as its counterpart the power to transfigure the common, the ordinary, into a radiant novelty. Like cells when seen through a microscope that suddenly spring to life.

But microscopic looking, as has been argued by philosophers of science, is inevitably also manipulating, transforming, the object seen.[8] The microscope—a baroque invention—is the instrument that both exalted the eye and demonstrated its impurity, its sticky involvement with the rest of the body. This condition of looking across difference in scale at the expense of retinal purity is endorsed, even foregrounded, in *Spider.* The work on scale, its destabilizing effect on the viewer's body, and the refocusing of attention away from what is large and important—here, say, the spider—to what is humbled yet takes over—the bottles—stipulates the conditions under which this work, and by extension, all works of visual art, can be viewed.

The use of objects from her own past, which Bourgeois introduced in the late 1980s and early 1990s, is a significant element in the architecture of a humble, nonspectacular yet intense sense of habitat. Not only do they invoke, through metonymic troping, the individual (the young girl growing up) life that encapsulated these tiny objects in a past which is narrativized into the present of viewing. Not only do these objects' metaphoric sense of the body's cells inscribe life within lifelessness and vice versa. The relentless coexistence of things infused with individuality and time, with mass-produced mute objects, also works at the intersection

8. See, in particular, Evelyn Fox Keller's fine essay (1999).

of individuality and collective existence. This, in turn, challenges the ideologies that have accrued to the notion of home itself. The home built here, and through which these bottles give us a guided tour, is not the cell of family life. While still a home, it criticizes the family home for not fulfilling its promise of safety and shelter, the pretext for its isolationism. What is deceptively promoted as the building block of the social fabric is open, permeable to the outside's penetration and the threat from the inside alike. For, as Teresa de Lauretis formulates it in a discussion of "family sickness," it is the family that is sick. Instead of rehearsing Bourgeois' anteriority narratives about childhood trauma, *Spider* is—as a built home—and embodies—as a permeable, closed-and-open structure—the family home, its problems, and an alternative to it. For, it is—and invites the viewers to take their seat or subject position—on the cutting edge that separates and binds public and private, mockingly demonstrating the futility of that indispensable illusion.[9]

This aspect of *Spider,* its foregrounding of the body's participation in viewing by way of its destabilization, is inherently narrativizing, but within a polemic against traditional conceptions of narrative. For it proposes viewing in an embodied and actualizing mode that reinvigorates narrative outside of the hang-up with importance, heroism, and individual mastery. In the same move, as it cements the building blocks together into an architectural work, this ungrandiose narrativity counters the seduction of monumentality. The association with memories of homeliness, unspectacular care, and unsatisfied ambition, said to inhere in Bourgeois' huge spiders, receives this polemical sense in relation to monumentality. Thus, by overruling the biographical anteriority narra-

9. See Teresa de Lauretis, "The Violence of Rhetoric."

tive, this polemic, debated on the level of architecturality, opens up the confinement it also induces. Here lies yet another theoretical proposition. Like Cotán's paintings, but in a different, not religious but more "intellectual" mode—visual thought—this work, to quote Bryson once again, aims to persuade vision "to shed its worldly education—both the eye's enslavement to the world's ideas of what is worthy of attention, and the eye's sloth, the blurs and entropies of vision that screen out everything in creation except what the world presents as spectacular" (64). Through its work with metaphor—which, as I will explain below, "embodies" this rhetorical figure—and specifically, with hyperbole, Bourgeois' work, indeed, puns on the very notion of the spectacular.

Presenting a spectacularly imposing spider, this artist offers no spectacle, for the spider cannot be seen at the same time as the cage to which it draws the viewer. The perfume bottles and the other objects from ordinary life are simply there, inscribing the sense of home on which the narrativity depends. Instead of spectacle, *Spider* offers only a stage on which, in which, the viewer is invited to act. Drama takes over, narrative becomes action, vision the play's actor. The director? Not the artist, but the work, in the dream of which the dreamer is just one player, among many others, an indispensable actor who does not hold the strings. The plot? Cells that compel a new kind of attention after the unlearning.

FIVE

> The most forgotten alien land is one's own body.
>
> WALTER BENJAMIN[1]

Cement of Cellular Stories

The word *cell*—the title is part of the work it names. The noun evokes blood and disease, body and life, but also prison, imprisonment, closure. "My body is my sculpture" (Bourgeois in Neri 1998: 83). By thus giving over her body to public access, her body merges with, becomes, her viewer's. *One and Others,* a sculpture in painted wood from 1955, proclaims this, as a theoretical object illuminating the *Cells* of which, like an architectural design, it projects an upside-down reversal (fig. 16). In *Spider,* the open door and the transparent cage don't allow me to forget this contagion by the work as body.[2]

Home, safe haven, and threat from inside; site of melancholia and desire. The artist talks about her mother as an assiduous spider but also about assaults from within the home on her dignity and sense of comfort. The uncanny bodily effects of the wavering scale, however, affect the viewer. And what we must contend with, then, is the

1. Benjamin wrote this in his essay on Kafka (1969: 132).
2. On the body in Bourgeois' work and its sexual aspects, which I will not develop here, see Meyer-Thoss 1992.

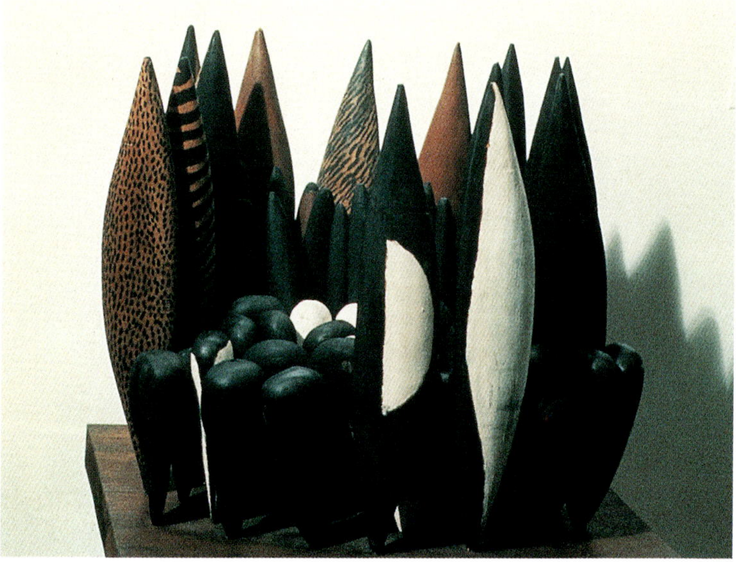

FIGURE 16 Louise Bourgeois, *One and Others,* 1955, painted wood, 18¼ × 20 × 16¼ in. Whitney Museum of American Art, New York. Photograph: Jeffrey Clements

way in which the *Cells,* and *Spider* in particular, do not reflect the maker's psyche but work the viewer's becoming. For, most effectively of all, these hollow forms allow *no exteriority.*

This is why the *Cells,* in addition to anything else, are primarily and profoundly architectures. But their architecturality is of an aspecific kind, qualified by "cellularity." This qualification, as a plea for a non-Vitruvian conception of architecture, is the proposition I draw in this chapter, from *Spider* as a theoretical object. What happens to and through the cellularity of *Spider* under the impact of the tiny bottles? These bottles and the need, in order to see them, to shed routine looking in favor of an unstable myopism, enforce a realization of how they represent as well as embody the visualization of life itself. Inert objects, they shimmer with the movement of the viewer's body. Thus they display, enact—as in drama—the dependency of cells on their environment, which they constitute in an ongoing process. Existing outside the viewer who remains outside, they also coalesce with that outside, which cannot function, qua viewer, without being physically affected by the bottles' tininess, which embodies their cell-dom.

Cells contain complete life; in that sense they are autonomous. Yet they are not. The multicellular organism—*One and Others*—can only develop, grow, if each cell continues to function within the organism, if it does its job according to the organism's rules. Between one cell and the others, the autonomy and the clutter, twentieth-century biology stands divided. Embryologists have asked the question "How does a germ cell develop into a multicellular organism?" This question was superseded by the geneticists' question: "Where, before that, did life begin?" They attributed all action to the gene. At the end of the century, the embryologists' question of differentiation was back on the agenda—this time of developmental biology. How does one cell, containing the principle of life, engage its others?[3]

If art as process, in the exhibition of it, is such a cellular community—where, as in an organism, differentiation happens—then each cell requires the willingness of its environment (its viewers) to be absorbed into its ever-extending multiplicity. The dependency-in-autonomy is enacted on all levels of scale. The tiny jars refer back to the great spider whose gigantic eggs lie on top of this *Cell,* the cage, but also inside it. Each part of the maze of the woven steel is a cell that needs cohesion with the other cells to exist as such. "Cellularity" stands for the wavering of scale in-

3. See Evelyn Fox Keller's brilliant account of the contribution made by choice metaphors on the actual scientific development of biology (1995). The quotation is from page 13 of that study.

volved in architecture according to this model, and foregrounded in *Spider.*

Between the multiform, *anexact yet rigorous* (Husserl's term) arrangement of bottles and bones and the regulated structure of the fabric in the tapestry fragments, another metaphoric relation establishes itself.[4] The woven steel, mediator between the inside it isolates and the outside it does not allow, is also the motivation of the metaphoric relationship between tapestry and bottles. This clutter of vicissitudinously differentiating cells, these patterns of regulated cells, are each other's signifiers. Among the levels of scale, a continuous process of expansion and incorporation takes place. This process is unspectacular, in the sense in which Bryson opposed narrative to still life. But it regains its narrativity once the viewer, humbled by the assault on her autonomy, steps into the dream and enacts her part—as just another cell. From element to whole, from cell to architecture, this process, this narrative, does not allow exteriority. Whether or not you actually go inside, you must act inside.

What, then, is this cellular play about? It's up to you, as long as you play it. For many plays can be activated at once. Round forms do not master beginning and ending. By making these forms crucial to the *Cells,* Bourgeois relinquishes mastery over her viewers, who are called upon to shed laziness and sloth and to improvise instead. Moreover, the *Cells* qua cells, self-contained as well as outgoing, blindly, do not distinguish interiority from exteriority. They exist in a process whose continuous transformation makes such a distinction moot. This particular play looks a bit like action theater in the 1960s. But this is not the only play.

4. In the words of Greg Lynn, Husserl introduced the concept in "The Origin of Geometry" (1936) to "describe forms which are neither exact (they cannot be reduced to mathematical statements) nor inexact (they can be measured with precision)" (1993: 61). See Derrida 1989.

Inside the cage-cell, the chair offers its tapestry, holding a "third-person narrative" narrated in the past tense. Old, now obsolete tragedies and comedies are just a bit too visible to be ignored. They are fragments of a cultural history not sitting mute as anterior but projecting, as fertile eggs, the future play enacted now, in *Jetztzeit.* The chair also offers itself, as in "first-person" narrative, as the site of subjectivity, remaining empty as it desires you to sit in it, inside the flat wall that the tapestry on the chair both decorates and represents. Desire, then, functions on the basis of the cell model, *One and Others,* pliable, engaging with other cells to maintain the organism.

To play your part in this play, consider *Cumul I* (fig. 17). On a different but also paradoxical scale, this white marble sculpture

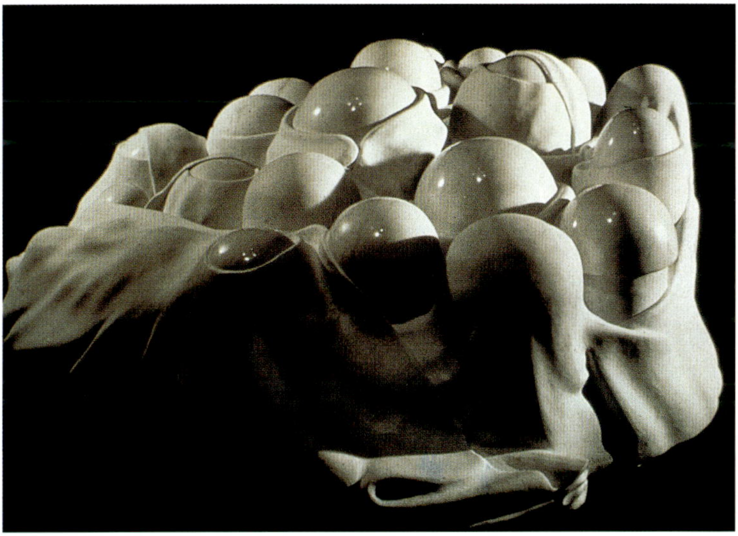

FIGURE 17 Louise Bourgeois, *Cumul I,* 1969, white marble, 22 3/8 × 50 × 48 in. Centre Georges Pompidou, Paris/Musée National d'Art Moderne/Centre de Création Industrielle. Photograph: Peter Moore

from 1969 possesses a multiple movement in its thrust, obliquely oriented toward the viewer. The ensemble of eggs peeping or bursting out of their cloth habitat explores interiority and exteriority in all its possible variations. The egg in the middle is the biggest one; it is the most ready to jump out and roll toward the viewer. But then, it cannot, can it? It will be stopped by the less advanced eggs, developing more slowly. Some of these become almost anthropomorphic, like Catholic nuns or Islamic women in various cultural covering garbs. The one that comes forward most directly toward the viewer is one of the smallest, one midway between inside and outside.

This luscious, deeply baroque sculpture also carries a friendly androgyny that plays with the cultural veneration for the icon of the phallus, winking and smiling almost tenderly at that icon's rigid need to show itself upright. Like *Blind Man's Buff* (1984, fig. 18), which is stylistically related, and *Janus in Leather Jacket* (1968) and *Janus Fleuri* (1968), *Cumul I* is decidedly but humorously antiphallic. It invokes both male and female bodily productivity in such a way that all are invited to participate, according to one's desires and possibilities. But as the marble cloth that covers the eggs emphasizes, in a manner similar to *Spider*'s nylon stockings around the eggs, this play cannot be played in isolation. The cloth delineates and protects, defines and confines the stage upon which the eggs are enabled to play.

Another play is on, simultaneously, the one in which we catch a glimpse of the single foot that marches through the meadow in the tapestry fragment behind the chair (fig. 5). Less benign, perhaps, this play threatens to cut off the foot that transgresses the boundary that separates inside from outside. It precludes forgetting the divisions and boundaries against which the work militates. The thrill of danger is lurking in this cut-off foot, but the

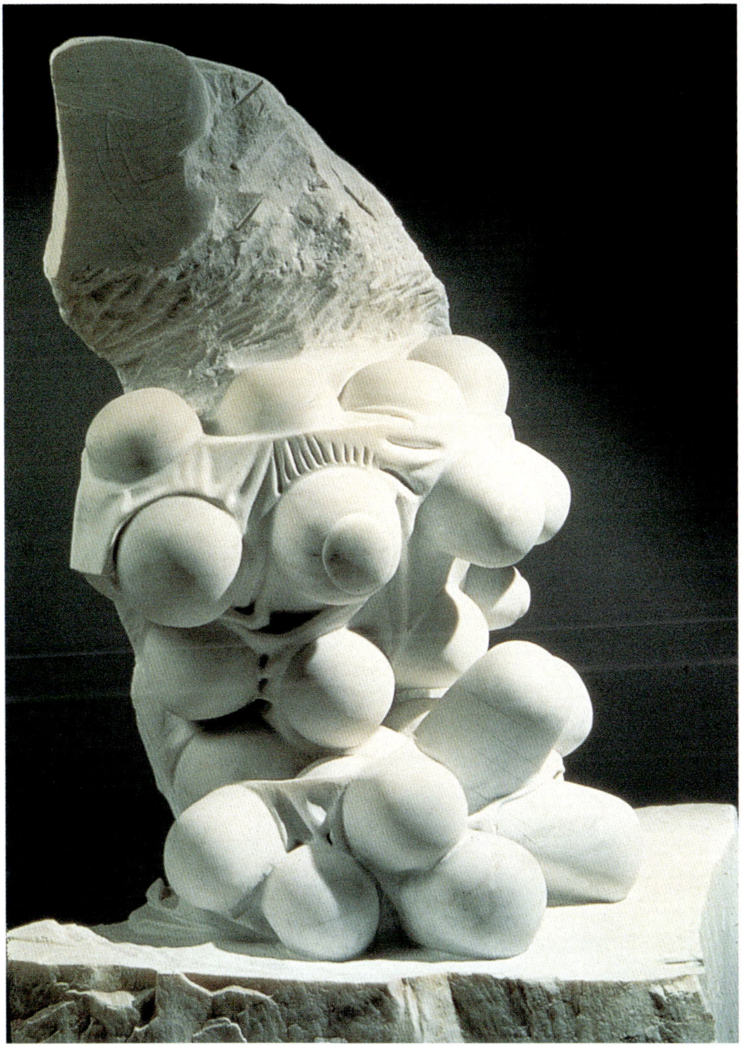

FIGURE 18 Louise Bourgeois, *Blind Man's Buff*, 1984, marble, 36½ × 35 × 25 in. Private collection, The Netherlands. Courtesy Galerie Karsten Greve, Koln/Paris/Milan/St Moritz. Photograph: Allan Finkelman

pieces offering the representations that trigger that thrill are too old, decidedly, to hamper enthusiasm and optimism.

What is the key to understanding this messy mix of stories within the cell? The key, visible, close-by, is out of reach, at least for those viewers confined to the outside. One story merges into another; this is what happens when cells coalesce. At times, the structured, rational aspect of the woven steel and woven tapestries has its remedial appeal—when scale's flippancy becomes a little sticky and when structure threatens to become invisible—allowing a sentimentalism of fluidity to overact. For, whereas the *Cells* solicit a conception of architecture based on internal differentiation rather than on a unified body, they neither idealize nor purify that alternative from the structuredness of its other.[5]

When one looks at a work of art, one is alone with it, in a confrontation with otherness. Cellularism—the visual thought offered by the *Cells* as concept, and by this *Cell* as spider body—holds a dynamic view of confrontation that reorients the very concept of otherness; from outside to parasitic, hence, differentiating within. This is an event, it says, not a state. An event not only of a one-to-one tension, perhaps polemic, but also an extension of self, and absorption into, and of, environment. The cell is a stage, theatrical, like the baroque it recalls and beckons. But it is also antitheatrical, mechanical; a monad containing the universe, yes, but also a waiting room where people stand, shuffle, are arranged or, precisely, not arranged, like clutter. A waiting room to which that one empty chair bears witness. A monad, but not a psyche; a possible world, but one that can only come true when

5. Fluidity is part and parcel of an alternative scientific paradigm that Bourgeois' work builds on. In the wake of vulgarizations in the kind of feminist theory proposed by Luce Irigaray (1974, 1977), it has become somewhat of an embarrassment. See, however, Christine Battersby's rather successful attempt to rehabilitate fluidity as a principle of identity (1998).

the viewer performs her role; a community, but not a family. This is the sense in which the confining prison of the cell also offers protection from the isolation of imprisonment.

If a building is a body, it is not a unified, symmetrical body. Bodies can be deformed, change, get sick. It is to be expected that as a whole, as a concept, the *Cells* involve, among their many plots, at least the story of disease. Discomfort, contagion, isolation; cancerous cells that don't obey the rules of the organism. *Cell I* (1991) makes isolating disease, isolation as disease, contagious.[6] By the same token, they involve life, promote it. No mood, however grim, is spared us; no meaning, however insistent, stabilizes. If the confining aspect of a cell-as-prison isolates, the wavering of scale guarantees that the cell as monad of life remains active in its coalescence with the viewer. Thus isolation is persistently absorbed within the narrative of continuity. *Viscosity,* that state between fluidity and solidity, may be the best word to characterize the narrativity of this stage on which the viewer must perform. It makes buildings that are bodies, but not idealized or stable ones.

Viscosity is visually represented in *Cumul I* by the miraculously effective cloth that covers the eggs. The space between the eggs does not show the limits of each. It is quite possible, this tantalizing cloth says, that beneath it the eggs are attached to one another, like the elements of a *rhizome.* As Christine Battersby (1998: 92) reminds us, this Deleuzian concept posits five features, which, I contend, are all represented in *Cumul I* and performed by *Spider.* The difference between their representation in marble and their performance in the *Cell*-as-stage turns the baroque sculpture from 1969 into the "egg" for an equally baroque architecture in 1997.

Deleuze and Guattari (1972, 1976, 1980) offer the metaphor of

6. See Crone and Graf Schaesberg 1998: 91–98 for a detailed reading of this early *Cell.*

the rhizome as an alternative to the limited one of structure, to emphasize that the object it describes consists of fragments that hang together, forming an ensemble characterized by heterogeneity. A rhizome is reducible to neither one nor the multiple. It is full of ruptures, breaks, and discontinuities. And it is a form of mapping rather than a trace. Battersby criticizes the degree to which the metaphor of the rhizome maintains "genetic continuities and origins in ways that bring back in the notion of a unified identity, or an originary parent or source" (192). Indeed, the distinction between eggs and fabric suggests rhizomic shape but denies its genetic unity.

On the level of representation, then, *Cumul I* is not quite rhizomic, but almost. Materially, however, it is. This is precisely what differentiates it, as a representation of such an ensemble carved out of a marble monolith, from *Spider,* where such genetic unification is no longer possible. Here, the unifying power resides with the viewer, who binds the fragments together within the building, on its stage, provisionally, and every time, differently. To the philosophers of the *rhizome,* then, *Spider* the theoretical object shows the way out of a remnant geneticism inherent in that concept. To the theorists of architecture, the cellularity of this "building" proposes a willful and systematic engagement with the uncertainty of scale that cellularism stands for. In retrospective response to *One and Others,* the double connectedness proposed there is here provided with a grounding in scale. Finally, these theoretical propositions only work if the emphasis in the notion of "work" as object—either sculpture or building—is shifted to the notion of work as affect, working on the viewer who is put in charge of the actual work of processing. Hesitantly, *Cumul I* yields to *Spider*'s viewers, entrusting them with a thrilling role to play.

SIX

A spider is merely an egg's way of making another egg.

PROVERB

Tales of Mother Spider

Earlier, I suggested that whereas the *Cells* preclude any traditional sense of narrative, the figurativity of the *Spiders* promotes it. This tension can be situated within the larger tension, often discussed, between figuration and abstraction. Bourgeois undermines the latter by establishing a tension where art-historical culture tends to see an opposition. She undermines that opposition in many ways, and one of these is to create the between-antinarrativism-and-narrative lure. I can now qualify this in a formulation that also shows the way out of the paradox while specifying its nature: the spiders promote a nostalgia for narrative—which is itself narrative.[1] But they withhold their tales. *Spider*'s spider is exorbitant in size, but its scale undercuts the illusionism of its representational mode. Yet that very scale also turns it into, say, a character from the animal fables we read when we were small. But the compulsion to fall back into a narrativity that the spiders promote, depends less on their hyperbolically figu-

1. On nostalgia, see Roth 1992 and Bal 1999: 64–75.

rative status—as humungous and illusionistic—than on something altogether different. They do so, not so much by a direct yet deceptive appeal to childhood memories, but because they embody vicissitudinous temporality. And it is within this vicissitudinous temporality that childhood memories impose themselves as mood while withholding themselves as narratives.

Just remember this: spiders can sit still for hours, in the middle of their web. Then, suddenly, they make their move. The spider on the ceiling of my bedroom showed up suddenly, without ever telling me where it came from. But it was always-already there, immobile. And when I least expected it to ever move again, it went scuttering away to another dark corner where it could frighten me. Whether one finds them frightening or comforting, spiders have an uncanny way of being in time.

This is also a function of the webs they weave. Their webs are sticky, but visually, they shine like silver. Or, they are old cobwebs in corners that look like balls of wool. Their look and feel are widely divergent. That is the "iconographic" source of the most strident mis-fit to the tactile eye—the contrast between the dry, rough, coarse fabric of the tapestry fragments and the glimmering look of the wire woven as cage. It also betokens that other strident mis-fit, between eye and skin. Our eyes say the steel is smooth, but our tactile memories of spider webs contradict that, unmasking the eye's habit of lying. The spider that remains exterior and interior to this *Cell* is constantly forgotten, too huge. But, as the entrance you pass through on your way to the cage, it is also inside it, at the center or core, where its body becomes another cell enclosing the eggs. Hence, when it is most forgotten, it shows up again, suddenly, like the spider that scared you so, or its sticky web.

According to many of her public statements, Bourgeois associates the spider with her mother: protecting, comforting, diligent, repairing.[2] Hovering over the cage, laying its eggs, it could very well be associated with such homeyness. Everything possible is done to prevent unambiguous creepiness from creeping in. But here, perhaps, the conflict between the concept of subjectivity in biographical and psychoanalytical criticism, respectively, is most acutely felt. Such statements are neither true nor false. They simply fall short of the work.

Biographical criticism—I have insisted on this before—would be inherently reductive. Here, another, theoretical reason can be alleged against biographism. Bourgeois' statements counter the theoretical proposition of at least this one of her works. For the explicit statement of the artist *about* her work cannot account for the spider's most decisive contribution to the work's *affect.* Whether "good" and motherly, or "bad" because scary, the spider operates through its imposition of a bodily involvement that destabilizes scale. Then, in the wake of that shaking, it is free to perform its imposition of *mood* within that body made vulnerable to the past, so that narrative can take its course. The spider *is* a home as well as stands over one, while at the same time she is inside it. Thus, she is the incarnation of Bourgeois' sculptural architecture. The best term for this specific sense of architecture is the title of Anthony Vidler's study, *The Architectural Uncanny. Spider* is both uncanny and motherly. Or rather, the uncanny, as is well known, is both strange, frightening, and motherly. For it recalls the home the mother's body once was, when we had no mastery whatsoever. In this sense, too, *Spider* as theoretical object militates against biographical anteriority narrative. But here, a subtle qualification further substantiates the logic of this polemic. If the spider of *Spider* represents the mother, diligence, impotence, cleanliness, and all that

2. She pronounces in that direction in the quotes throughout Gorovoy, Asbaghi, Herkenhoff 1997. See also Kotik 1994.

comes with motherhood as qualified in a spiderly way, the deep anteriority involved in that association harks back to a stage so anterior that it precedes awareness as a form of mastery. The architectural uncanny, in other words, undermines the very representational makeup on which it is based.

And then, of course, we are thrown into psychoanalysis, and *its* anteriority. Psychoanalytic criticism would ask how the weight of unconscious memories can remain once insight has replaced them. I am not questioning the artist's insistence on a positive mother image, there where ambivalence seems to be inevitable. Rather, the relevance of the artist's biography must yield to the presentness, the *Jetztzeit,* the dynamic power the work imposes. The relevance of her psyche, even those aspects of it that remain unconscious, must yield to the mood where the viewer's unconscious meets the work's power, in a pastness of each viewer's memories that comes *after,* not before, the encounter.

In other words, anteriority falls apart; the work is greater than the subject who made it. For some viewers, the spider may represent the deadly threat associated—in the vulgarization of surrealism—with the *Black Widow,* who eats her mate. For others, she may simply stand for disgust, when memories of sticky webs predominate, and inflect the sight of her, despite the cleanliness accorded spiders in natural history books. If you have ever been threatened, or experienced the sense of being threatened by a spider—or by your mother, for that matter—no amount of reassurance will help. The spider also represents, in this sense, a *screen memory* of the Freudian kind. To allege an example from my own affective response to this work: I could not help but be struck, quite forcefully, by the fear I once experienced when I was seriously threatened by a gigantic, dangerous white spider. *Spider's* spider is black, or at least, dark. But its size reanimated that enormous monster on that site in eastern India. Its color was superposed on that earlier memory, which was, nevertheless, itself a latecomer in my life, childhood memories of spiders of normal size that posed no threat at all. Why was I still afraid?

It makes no sense to interpret my fears for your benefit. I evoke them to drive the point home that is at stake in the theoretical object. "Memoriness" is not, cannot be, "about" anyone's specific memories. This is why the spider of *Spider* must withhold specific tales. Of course, I am not going to tell you what mood this spider ought to instill in you, or absorb you in. All I have at my disposal to state my case is my own, not Bourgeois', memories of mood. The point is, precisely, that it must remain undecided, for each event of viewing, each act of looking and experiencing this spider-cell catches the moment in its sticky web, so that the *Jetztzeit* is drawn out into long threads. Like the ribs of spider webs, the threads are centrifugal; they each go in a different direction. We all have different memories, memory-cells that coalesce into a new organism. But, whereas the specific mood, the particular narrative of each reactivation of memory cannot be determined, the narrativity the spider emanates by means of mood—its virtual viscosity—is unavoidable; there, not in the specific plots, lies the paradoxical power of the work to *impose free, individual* tales of the past on each of us. This is how, at the end of the day, it is *Spider,* not the spider, who tells the stories and lays the eggs that breed spiders. In this sense only, there is a mother busying about in this work, building the rooms in which spiders can sit.

SEVEN

Fragmented Bodies

For cells, as for computers, memory makes complex programs possible; and many cells together, each one stepping through its complex developmental control program, generate a complex adult body. BRUCE ALBERTS[1]

One of the crucial meanings of the *Cells* as theoretical objects is to resist "translation," both of iconographic elements and of psychoanalytic motifs. Hence, they tease the viewer's interpretive lust. Each *Cell* is a self-contained habitat, and each is inhabited by isolated objects. These objects resist interpretation in themselves, but they also fail to serve as a handmaiden for the construction of a unified, coherent whole. Again, *Spider* makes this paradoxical point perhaps more emphatically, more self-reflexively, than all the other *Cells*. The predominant element in *Spider* is fragmentation incarnated: the fragments of tapestry that are hung, stretched, framed, as just that, as bits and pieces of tapestry, decorations on the wall, the wall they cover, decorate, and constitute.

These cloth fragments are shards of the past: of the child watching, of the adolescent working in her parents' workshop, of the eighteenth century from which they came, of the Renaissance, which they represent, of

1. From Alberts et al. (1989: 902), quoted by Keller (1995: 114).

antiquity whose architecture the represented Renaissance represented. Fragments, too, are the working elements of the restorer, the archaeologist, and, if Freud's fond use of archaeological metaphors is any indication, of the psychoanalyst as well as the dreamer. Fragments stand for the whole they once were and can become again—albeit only anachronistically—through restoration. In this conception, the use of fragments suggests a nostalgic recall of the wholeness—the unified body, the continuous timeline, the architectural structure of perfect balance. Fragments, then, are also anteriority incarnated. Or are they?[2]

Affixed to the wall of the cage, the fragments partake of the architecture, the building, or, more precisely, the building blocks, of an alternative, coalescent, cellular architecture that the *Cells* also appear to be. The concept of cell offers an alternative model for the organization of space "based on the behavior of local particularities (base matter) as they contribute to the composition of provisional unities (bodies) from the bottom up, describing various degrees of cohesiveness and unity within bodies."[3] Beyond and through the iconographic symbolism of cells that cannot be ignored, the multiple fragmentation that is a key element of the meaning of the concept of the cell is also, and perhaps primarily, a statement on space.

By means of the fragmented quality that allows inside and outside of the built space to become porous, *Spider* achieves something similar to what Francis Bacon, according to Ernst van Alphen (1992), achieves in some of his paintings: "The difference between inside and outside is challenged here, and that challenge is posed

2. A propos of *The Destruction of the Father,* Mignon Nixon speaks of the withdrawal from language as "not . . . so much private or personal as *resistant.*" This seems an adequate formulation, also, to point to what I would call the "social affect" of the fragments as interpretive teases.

3. These are the words with which Greg Lynn begins his articulation of an alternative conception of architecture (1993: 61).

when body and space form one continuous field of dispersed elements."[4] Whereas Bacon questions space, its wholeness and its delimitations, within two-dimensional paintings, Bourgeois does this by means of the inextricable integration of a three-dimensional structure, "decorated" as well as walled-in by fragmented narratives through whose holes we can look in. As a result, to quote Van Alphen again: "Figural, represented space cannot be distinguished clearly from literal, primary space. The space of representation is an ambiguous zone. Just as the line between inside and outside cannot be drawn, so also the distinction between model and representation is fluid" (152). The result, Van Alphen continues, is a "tangle of ontological dimensions." *Spider,* building its space with found objects and fragments, does not contain a single ambiguous or blurred line. Visually, all is clear. Yet, by using means that are more literally building blocks, the work produces a similar tangle of ontological dimensions. For *Spider*'s work with fragmentation and layering, the consequence of this tangle is that it irrevocably catches the viewer in its web.

Hence, the architectural and the narrative need each other to come about. As a truly Derridean case of parergon, the pieces of tapestry cannot be seen separately from the wall, for they are part of it. Neither interior nor exterior, they are what they decorate. Flat surfaces, they constitute the hollow space they contradict. Thus they behave like the spider herself. They also do what the fragment to the left of the chair represents: they contradict the square, structural, rigid character of architecture as it is imagined in culturally predominant fictions such as Renaissance linear perspective.[5]

4. Van Alphen (1992: 146) makes this argument in his chapter "Bodyscapes" (114–63), which as a whole is extremely relevant to the discussion at hand.

5. See, on the deceptions of perspective, Hubert Damisch 1994. Greg Lynn (1993) offers an insightful alternative basis for the architectural imagination, where not the unified, well-proportioned

Sitting at the border of the cell, these fabrics stand guard against exteriority. This is one reason why they cannot be expected to cover the entire surface of the wall. If they did, they would, paradoxically, ward off the viewer's gaze. But part of the work's point is precisely to inscribe, inside the viewer's body, the tension between being shut out of and being let into the cage. But even when this paradox is absorbed, the work keeps us suspended in confusion yet again, for these scraps of pastness remain stubbornly fragmented. They do not ask for restoration, even if they did do this in the workshop from which they came. Not only are they emphatically not whole; they have holes in them that point to the hand that made them—made them as such: full of holes.

One such hole was made by the artist's mother. She cut out the genitals of a putto in one of her tapestries to accommodate rather prudish customers. Or so the story goes (fig. 19). The gesture of literal castration for the good of the family business is just one example of the extreme and daring ambivalence that pervades Bourgeois' work when it makes explicit reference to her mother. This is the same mother, mind you, who mended and healed, comforted and protected, in her remembered state of spider. But since this work's theoretical tenet is to counter the reductive psychoanalytical practice that such an interpretation requires, the notion of castration as a specific psychoanalytic concept must cautiously be kept at bay, at arm's length, although not out of sight. Instead, making holes is offered here as something that cannot be read "off the page." For, regardless of why the hole was made,

---

body is the model, but a viscous body modeled according to the cell's propensity to shape and adapt to, invade and absorb, the environment. Lynn's view of urban planning and architecture fits "squarely," to use an extraordinarily unfitting metaphor, with Bourgeois' *Cells,* whose thrust as theoretical objects could have helped him to make his point more concretely.

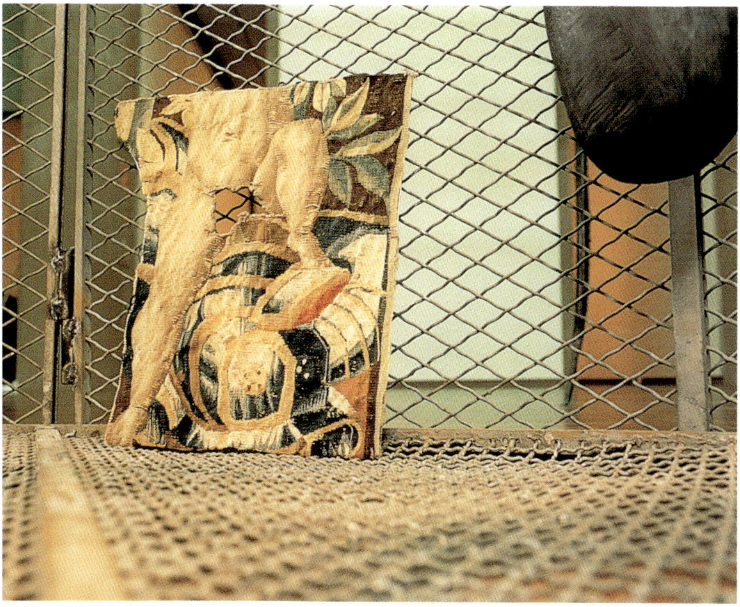

FIGURE 19 Louise Bourgeois, *Spider* (detail: *putto* with genitals cut out), 1997, steel and mixed media, 175 × 262 × 204 in. Courtesy Cheim & Read, New York. Photograph: Marcus Schneider

when, and by whom, and for whatever overt or unconscious purpose, its signifying effect is to multiply the layers of pastness as an effect—hence, a posterior moment—of the work.

That particularly notorious hole also indicates that fragmentation is not simply a state of the ancient tapestry. It is also an activity, subjectively informed, subjectively coproduced. If the artist took up where her mother left off, so the viewers take up where the artist left off. The act of fragmentation partakes of the complex and multifarious act of involved vision that *Spider* requires. Rather than reading the hole "off the page," as castration, it must be read as an integrated element in the visual discourse and its foregrounded rhetoric that beckons the viewer in. A rhetorical reading, therefore, seems more suitable here.

Metonymically related to a past it projects within the present of looking, the hole is also a synecdoche of the fragmentation of all these shreds and scraps. As synecdoche, it articulates fragmentation's defining function in the irresistible narrativity of *Spider*. But its operation is more complex than the sheer mention of such rhetorical figures might suggest. Instead of conjuring up terms used mostly for the analysis of language, I propose calling upon this hole to flesh out these rhetorical terms in their visual specificity. For whatever else the tapestry fragments are, they are real, material leftovers of a past that, through their doing, is here, with us, in the *Jetztzeit* of this work. Materiality, then, is their language.

Metonymy binds the hole's materiality to another materiality that coexists with it—in time, space, or logic, or, as the case may be, in all three. In time, the hole is bound to the artist's past, childhood, mother, work, even if any specific reference is bracketed. Yet, this is no anteriority narrative. Instead of presenting us with an explanatory past, it frames that past and displays its framing. The edges of this hole are different, more recent, than the edges of the other pieces' boundaries. As such, they are emphasized by the repetition of piercing in the steel plate on which the fragment is mounted.

In space, it lets our gaze into the cage, through that particular, disturbing hole. And if you are inside, you can look out through it. Do you really want to look through this figure's genitals? But can you resist doing it? Well, you didn't, did you, when you boldly approached the cage from between the spider's legs. Just look back, after looking in. And then, if you go inside, in body or only visually, the hole attracts and forces you to look out again. But across the hole runs a cross, of the woven steel of the cage, a symptom-sign of censorship.[6]

And in logic, finally, when we peep through it, our look is facilitated, caused by the act—of making an artwork, or holes—of fragmentation. From the abstraction of an exterior disembodied logic, the hole, while only being negatively defined as absence, moves logic and its major player, causality, into concreteness. Given the extremely bodily mode of looking that this work solicits, primarily by means of its work with scale, the fragmentation, then, is contagious.

It suddenly shifts our rhetoric from metonymy to synecdoche. If the hole stands for the whole of which it is a part—as the figure of synecdoche has it—then this hole represents wholeness as hole, caused by and resulting in fragmentation. The emptiness at the center of the subject's body, here signified in this small hole, refers us back to the empty chair in which the director of the play did not sit—so that we can sit there, virtually. But before the work extends the discussion to other aspects of fragmentation, a third figure of rhetoric beckons from the wing. Metaphor, the mother of rhetoric, must relieve the anxiety this web of implications might arouse. For, whereas metonymy and synecdoche are grounded in material contiguity, metaphor allows escape into a flight of the imagination. It takes us out of the sticky concreteness of metonymy and synecdoche. One thing stands for another, which is absent. Or so it seems.

Metaphor is the figure that establishes partial similarity, hence,

6. A symptom is an involuntary, unintentional sign. When the leaves of a tree turn yellow, the color change is a sign of the changing season. But no one designs that sign. The term "symptom" has no medical connotations, but obviously it lends itself for use in medical diagnosis, where the doctor reads the signs of disease that no one intends. Similarly, Bourgeois' use of the castrated putto is a sign, but the visibility of the "x" behind it is an accident that can receive meaning in the context of the work; hence, it is a symptom.

similarity-in-difference, between the present sign and its absent counterpart. But here, too, Bourgeois will not let convention dictate her concepts. It has been pointed out that her *Cells* are "the very embodiment of metaphorical thinking" (Crone and Graf Schaesberg 1998: 90). But this is a very paradoxical, if not metaphorical, way of speaking. The *Cells* do not so much offer metaphors as particles that can be isolated and interpreted, such as the metaphor of "cell" for life, disease, the infinitely small, confinement, protection, for what have you. When the *Cells* embody metaphors, they are such figures. This sounds precisely right to me.

Except that it makes no sense, unless we revise, through *Spider* as theoretical object, the concept of metaphor. No longer an escape from literal, material reality, metaphors à la Louise literalize their own name. *Meta-phorein* means transference, as in "translation." We know this concept in its guise of "transference" from psychoanalytic theory. There, transference points to the process in which the analysand projects on the analyst her phantoms from the past. The point being, precisely, that these phantoms stand up in the present, so that they can be effectively dealt with. Transference is a narrative of performance that draws the past into the present in order to revise the play. But transference is a transfer in the material sense as well; any vacationer to Greece has seen the word "metaphor" on moving vans.[7]

The literal sense of metaphor is to transfer onto the viewer what the object is, says, and does. In the case of the fragments of tapestry that characterize *Spider*, these mediators between inside and outside that contaminate the viewer, are not conceptual as opposed to material, but conceptual in their very materiality. With

7. On metaphor and the epistemological ambivalence with which it is often regarded, see Bal 1994.

their frayed edges, bearing witness to their ancient history and the pastness this history carries with it, metaphorizing, into the present, they conceptualize metaphor in a hyperbolic materiality. From the present in which they exist, the fragments, like the bodies they activate, beckon to the past, to become part of the *Jetztzeit* in which they—and it—matter.

EIGHT

Beckoning Bernini

> ... the necessity and proper use of anachronism in art history.
>
> HUBERT DAMISCH[1]

The materialization of metaphor, that traditional figure of escape from matter, is *Spider*'s theoretical contribution to rhetoric. The integration of transference and translation contaminates the latter with the projective and subjective quality of the former. Through the deployment of fragmentation as a practice of such transference/translation, Bourgeois' metaphoric performance definitively undermines anteriority narrative. In *Spider,* Bourgeois does this most emphatically by means of the "castrated," mother-invoking *putto.* This *mise-en-abyme* of Bourgeois' metaphoring will transfer us across historical divides, from the end of the twentieth century to the beginning of the seventeenth.

The aspect of the *Cells* that the fragments—but before and after them, the spider of *Spider*—most emphatically foreground is this play with layers, which unveils the ultimate emptiness, the absence of a hard core, to which they might wrongly be reduced. This emptiness defines architecture as sculpture's other and sculpture's

1. In Careri 1995: viii. Damisch is referring to Careri's invocation of Eisenstein to understand Bernini.

house. Emptiness, the absence of the Renaissance vanishing point or the transcendental signifier of unification and visual power, is the key meaning of the baroque *fold.* And when it comes to the avid iconographic eye that is being teased in *Spider,* the concrete figure in which this emptiness takes hold is, precisely, the baroque *putto.* The *putto* whose genitals are lacking: that figure of emptiness may be the work's wink to the baroque—critical, traversing,[2] and surpassing, all with a smile. But while smiles may fit baroque lightness of being, they don't preclude the most serious, crucial engagement between a contemporary and a historical work. Here, a single figure as mise-en-abyme of a whole series of works, the *Cells,* which completely rethink sculpture, establishes, through the figure of the *putto* and the metaphor of the emptiness at its body's center, a crucial *preposterous* connection. To understand this connection, I invoke here the eminent practitioner of sculpture as the most quintessentially baroque art, Bernini.

Not only in her sculpture *Baroque* (1970) and a number of almost programmatically baroque sculptures such as *Cumul I* (1969) did Bourgeois engage the baroque sculptor *par excellence.* She also did so in *Homage to Bernini* (1967), which can be seen as a prototype of the *Cells,* or even, in its egglike shape, of *Spider* specifically (fig. 20). The triangular relationship between Bernini, *Homage to Bernini,* and *Spider* stands here for the double commitment of *Spider* as theoretical object to propose a radically new conception of sculpture-as-architecture and through its meta-historical thrust as a plea for an engaged relationship to the past that is one neither of influence nor reconstruction.

2. Traversing, here, also alludes to the psychoanalytical concept of traversal. Catherine Lord (1999) discusses and deploys this concept in an analysis of literary interactions among George Eliot, Virginia Woolf, and Jeanette Winterson. This study of relations of intimacy among artists across history is highly relevant here.

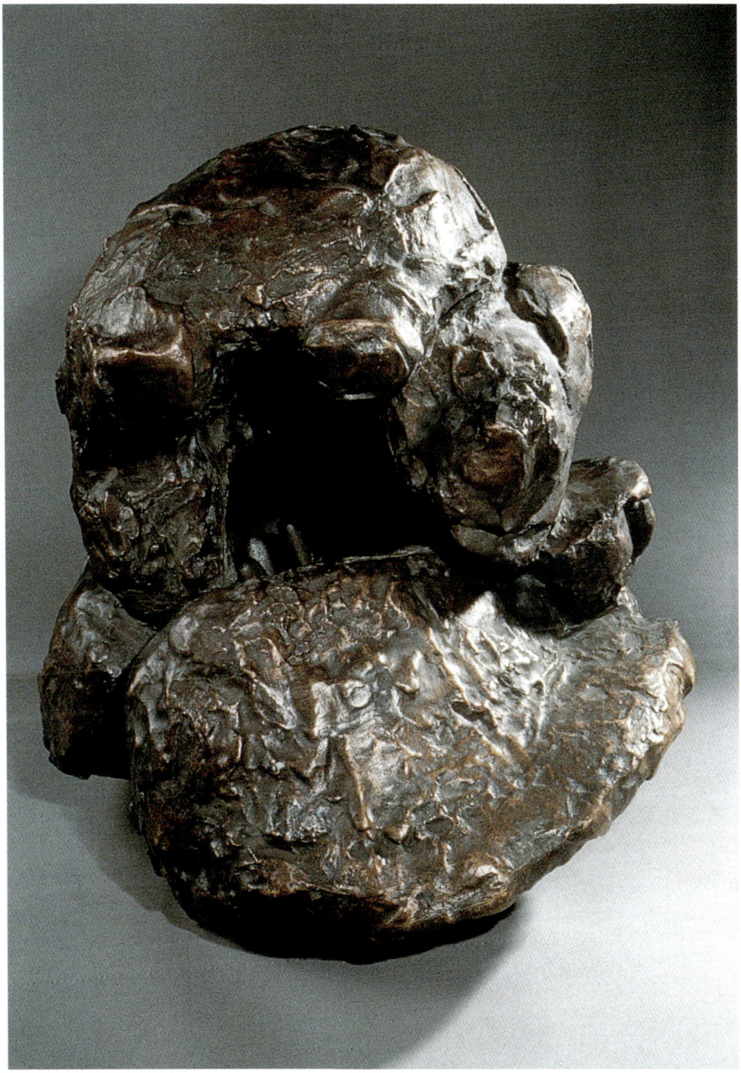

FIGURE 20 Louise Bourgeois, *Homage to Bernini,* 1967, bronze, 21½ × 20 × 23 in. Courtesy Cheim & Read, New York. Photograph: Allan Finkelman

In chapter 3, I mentioned Bernini's *Apollo and Daphne* as an example of a visual work that was read, literally, from a page of Ovid's *Metamorphoses.* The story of the transformation of a threatened, fleeing woman into a rooted laurel tree was bound to challenge a sculptor whose ambition it was to tell stories in stone. Prefacing and concluding the discussion by way of three other works by Bourgeois—*Baroque, Homage to Bernini,* and *Femme-Maison* —I will discuss *Spider*'s critical commentary on three of Bernini's most keenly narrative sculptures as an example of the way in which Bourgeois' *Spider,* and by extension, the *Cells,* not only undermine traditional narrative but do so from within that tradition. Both the works from the past and Bourgeois' responses to them emerge enriched from the encounter, to become the fullest possible integration of sculpture into architecture. Thus, they complete Bernini's project, by pushing his work beyond its limits yet staying on his side, pursuing the very project that Bernini himself so keenly pursued.

Bernini's *Apollo and Daphne,* one of his early successes, is self-reflexive about narrativity in the sense that it proclaims that sculpture can perform the paradoxical feat of preserving movement within stillness (fig. 21). Ovid's story is not only *transformed* from its literary narrativity *into* a visual object that retains its movement; it is a story *about* such a transformation. Daphne's existence as a tree fixes her in one place but allows her to continue moving there, and to grow. Where her hair sprouts leaves, the sculptor struggled to maintain continuity between the wind-blown hair and the stiff laurel leaves that begin to clutter their ends. Roots seem to stream out of her toes like water. Differing registers of the fluidity of live matter are juxtaposed.

But the relevance of Bernini's work for *Spider* becomes most visible at the site where the tree's bark begins to cover the woman's

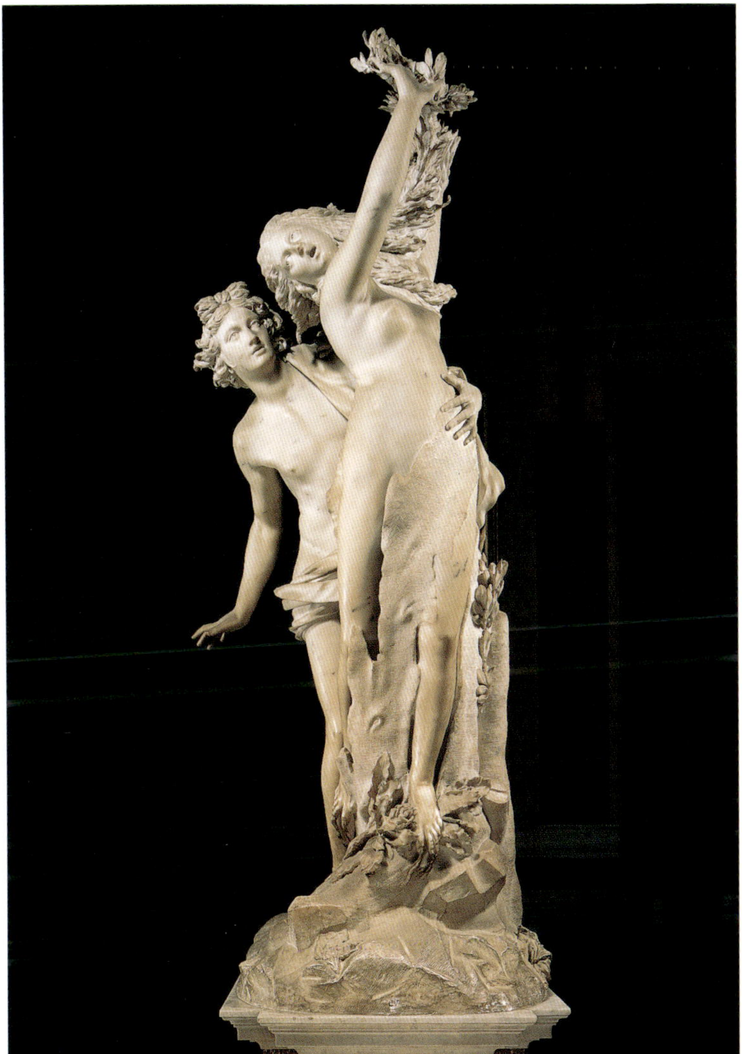

FIGURE 21 Gianlorenzo Bernini, *Apollo and Daphne,* 1622–25, marble, Villa Borghese, Rome. Photograph: Scala/Art Resource, New York

soft skin. Over and between her legs, a detached, separate layer of bark heightens the paradox. Qua marble, as an opaque, solid, hard material, the layering of surfaces rightly earned Bernini admiration. The layer of bark is both thin and coarse—just like bark. It contrasts with the soft skin that covers the flesh about to disappear into wood. But the sculptor can only acknowledge, visually, that body and skin, inner substance and outer layer, must remain separate. The bark, incidentally, covers Daphne's genitals. But it covers them with a detached layer, like a piece of fabric, of clothing, a decoration.

Where Bernini covered the woman's genitals, Bourgeois—or her mother—cut out the genitals of that quintessentially baroque male figure of the *putto.* Iconographic reversal seems, here, ludicrously incidental, unless it is a caricature, part of Bourgeois' mildly mocking smile. But as *Homage to Bernini* indicates, Bourgeois has other ways of addressing Bernini. The hole at the center of the *putto* can be illuminated by the latter work's addition of bark to *its* central emptiness. Inside the coarse hollow shape, a few tiny, shiny poles pop up like miniature male genitals, fingers, pods, or plants—or, again, mocking all of the above—inside a gigantic hollow space that could be a house, or a gigantic womb.

Bernini's project was clearly invested in the narrativity of transformation. In *Apollo and Daphne* this issue of transformation was still located quite precisely in the area of the body that Bourgeois' *putto* recalls—as if that poor creature is being punished for Daphne's plight. Then, mid-career (1647–52), in *The Ecstasy of Saint Teresa,* Bernini tried his hand at a religious version of a similar narrative of transformation (fig. 22). Capturing the moment of ecstasy of the sixteenth-century Spanish mystic, he again made the transformation itself the subject of his narrative in stone. This time his struggle with layering was more successful. Rather

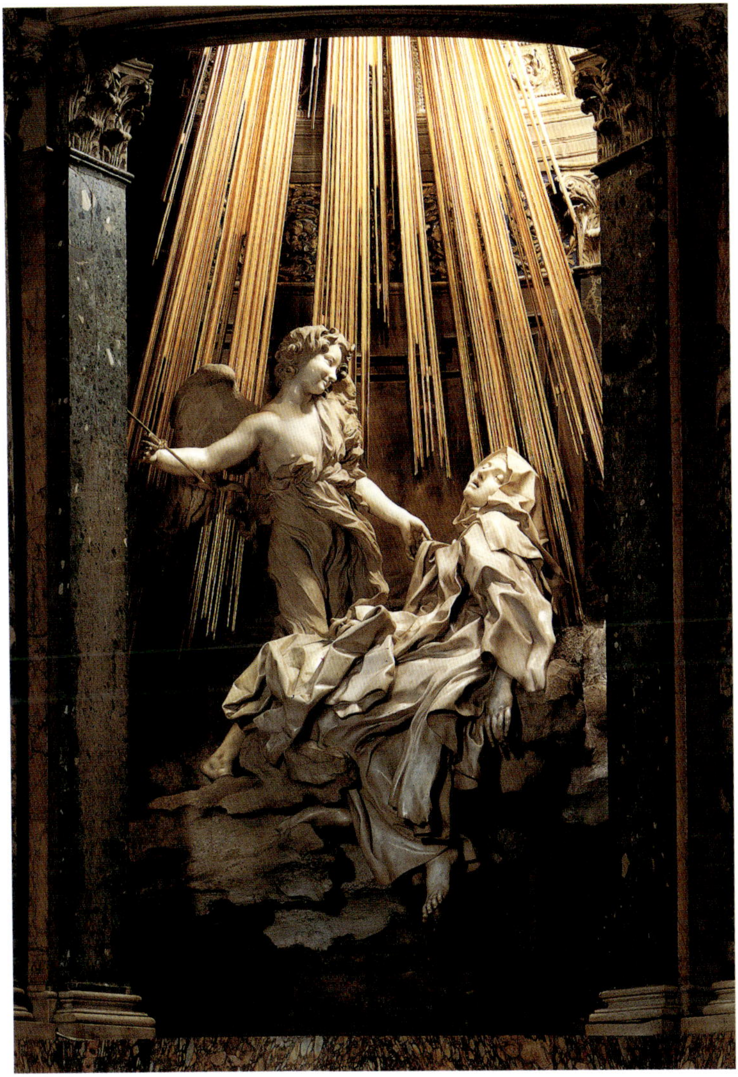

FIGURE 22 Gianlorenzo Bernini, *The Ecstasy of Saint Teresa* (detail), 1647–52, marble, Santa Maria della Vittoria, Rome. Photograph: Scala/Art Resource, New York

than being genitally localized, this struggle problematized localization itself. The transformation of Teresa's body set on divine fire by the arrow thrust into her breast by an angel this time is literally embodied. Teresa's body, curved in an obliquely reclining S-shape, takes the shape of a flame. But her body's inside cannot be distinguished from its outside.

In his 1972–73 seminar, published as *Seminar 20*, Jacques Lacan demonstrates the blindness that comes with obsession when he claims that Teresa's *jouissance* is a matter of her desire to be penetrated again and again (*encore*) by God, the transcendental phallus.[3] Bernini's sculpture—and Teresa's writings—however, suggest that the ecstasy is due to, or rather consists of, literal ec-stasy: the propagation of the fire of love from inside out, so that Teresa's skin, that outer limit of the body, partakes of it; hence, her body's limits are themselves no longer limits. Her garments, the lusciously folded drapery that iconographically marks the sculpture as baroque, equally transforms into flames (Lavin 1980). Her whole body becomes a flame: each part of it, of its cover, its surface but beneath which nothing else remains, becomes a flame; fire comes to overrule previous shapes. The transformation, here more aptly called transfiguration, is total.

Transfiguration, including its collusion with death, is not unrelated to what Georges Bataille called *alteration.*[4] According to Krauss' account of it, this concept simultaneously grasps two totally different logics. The first logic is that of decomposition, the blurring of boundaries through matter's tendency to dissipate. The second is what we would today call "othering": the logic of radical distinction. The two meet where death decomposes the body and

3. See, for the relevant fragments, Mitchell and Rose, eds., 1982: 137–61.

4. Rosalind Krauss uses Bataille's term to elaborate a concept for the analysis of surrealism beyond the formalist argument that considered surrealism not formally innovative. See Krauss 1999: 7–8.

transforms the former subject into a soul, ghost, or spirit. The two meet, that is, in a transfiguration that both "melts" the body and elevates it to sanctity. This is why flames can so aptly replace decomposition. But flames themselves are in movement, hovering, as J. L. Austin said when he made fire the key metaphor for his speech-act theory of language, between thing and event.[5] The resolution of the hesitation between narrative movement and still visuality could, therefore, be nowhere better shaped than in this all-consuming fire.

The integration of Teresa's inside and outside fires can also be seen as programmatic of a sculpture that integrates within itself the architecture that houses it. And, conversely, the sculpture is integrated within a chapel in which the viewer must stand in order to see it. This integration is precisely part of the challenge posed by the *Cells,* where it is so dramatically radicalized that the two domains become one. One of Bernini's later sculptures—like the *Teresa* representing a holy woman in the unified composition of a chapel—pushes the inquiry into narrative sculpture even further, and does so, again, within the unification of sculpture and architecture. The *Blessed Ludovica Albertoni* (1671–74) represents the moment of death and ascension in the same double movement (fig. 23). The body reclines, or rather, lays down her head, just now bent backwards, as the holy woman expires. Out of the unity of the garments and the body, the small but insistent sign of the hand pressing the breast offers a metonymically motivated metaphor. The colored folds of the bedding under her body indicate a diagonal movement upwards. Most strikingly, though, the

5. Speech-act theory with its insistence on the meaning-producing effect of utterance, remains a compelling framework within which to rethink contemporary art. Austin's theory (1975) has been subject to (failed) attempts to "normalize" it, as Shoshana Felman (1983) argues. For Felman, incidentally, seduction is the paradigmatic speech act.

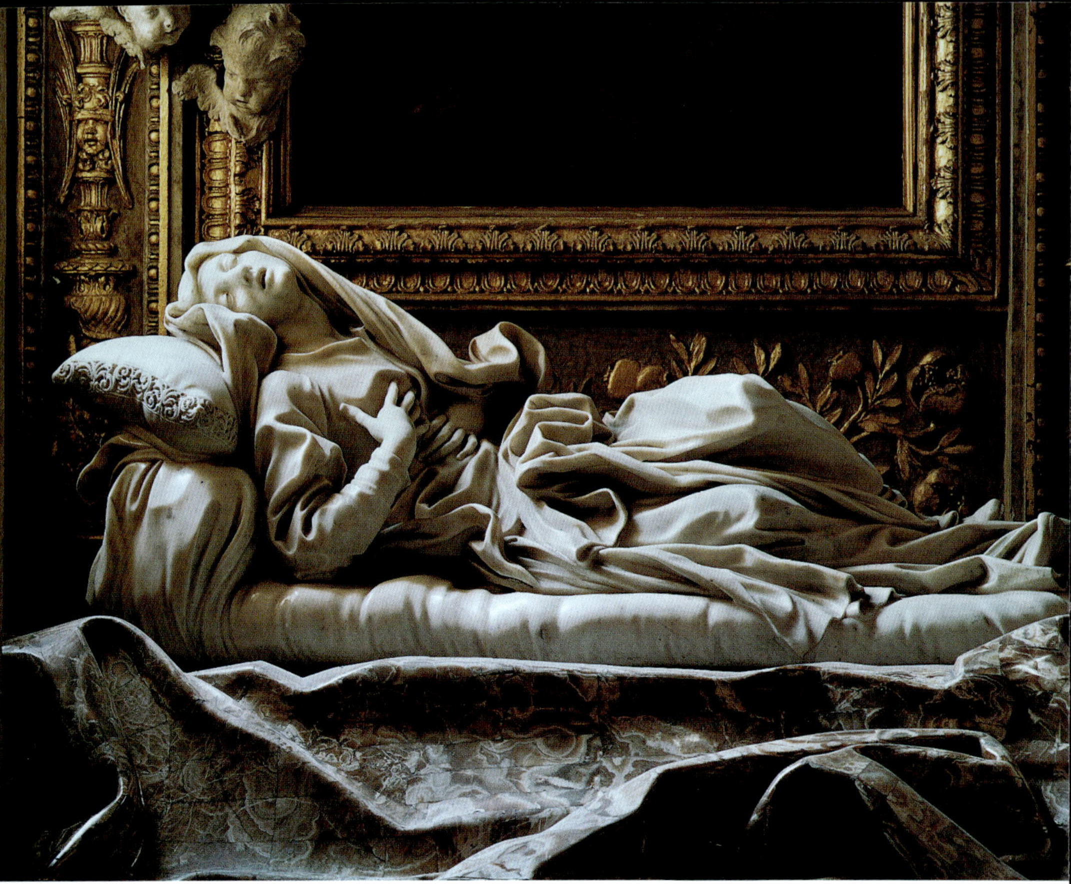

FIGURE 23 Gianlorenzo Bernini, *Blessed Ludovica Albertoni,* 1671–74, marble, San Francisco a Ripa, Rome. Photograph: Scala/Art Resource, New York

folds of the garment, so completely covering her body that it can be said to constitute it, in the same way the spider constitutes the cage of *Spider,* stand so erect that they pull the heavier body up.

As if in reminiscence of Daphne's covered genitals, the drape extends horizontally between Ludovica's legs. But that extended fold ends just where it becomes a bit too iconic of the slit it is allegedly covering. This fold is absorbed, elevated, if not *aufgeheben,* in a series of short but firmly erect folds that pull the holy woman up, body and soul. These folds, I cannot help but notice, resonate with the tiny poles inside Bourgeois' *Homage to Bernini.*[6]

These three sculptures—*Apollo and Daphne, The Ecstasy of Saint Teresa,* and *Blessed Ludovica Albertoni*—in another kind of dialectic, stand here for three moments in Bernini's exemplary exploration of sculptural narrative and its inevitable move toward integration into architecture. Bourgeois' *Spider* addresses them all. *Daphne,* taken from a pagan story transformed by this Christian sculptor, was still subject to a division between inner body and outer layer, so that her transformation confined her to the fragmentation to which a subject remains condemned when exteriority and interiority are divided. Teresa's transformation into a voluptuous fire consumed her entirely. She escapes fragmentation, division, but at the cost of her total absorption into the otherness of her desire. Ludovica, whose marble body bending backwards resists a too-easy consummation, insists on her body's bodiliness. To the extent her head resists elevation, it proclaims that her body, qua body—sexed female—be accepted in the transformation. Like Christ himself, she will ascend whole, in the *aufgeheben* materiality of flesh beyond corruption. Crucially, for the issue of Bourgeois' architecturality, these differences are also reflected in the material existence of Bernini's sculptures: in their relationship to real space, hence, to architecture. Bernini's two holy women are integrated within a chapel. Daphne, although suffering the excessive bodily proximity of Apollo's desire for her, stands alone when facing the viewer. Like the small vanguard egg in *Cumul I* that drags heavy folds of fabric below it like a bride drags her veil, Daphne, with the front of her body, her most "layered" past, reorients the viewer,

6. On Bernini's work in general, see Wittkower 1955 and Scribner 1991; on *Apollo and Daphne,* Herrmann Fiore 1997. On the *Blessed Ludovica,* see Perlove 1990 and, most relevantly, Careri's brilliant study of the integration of sculpture within architecture, which he discusses in terms of montage (1995).

who cannot quite live down the illusion that this whirling sculpture is "really" round in the same sense as Bourgeois' *Spider.* The narrative holds the viewer riveted, glued to a linearity that inexorably leads to the front of Daphne's transforming body. Here narrative supersedes sculpturality precisely to the extent that the form remains suspended in relation to real space, encouraging projection rather than absorption. By making her narrativizing spider both outer limit and inner center, Bourgeois provides Bernini with a radical alternative.

As Giovanni Careri pointed out, the sculpture of the Blessed Ludovica, on the other hand, formally but also in its meaning and the impact of its narrative, cannot be considered in isolation from the chapel as a whole. The chapel beckons the viewer in; the sculpture, in spite of its situatedness beyond the threshold the viewer cannot overstep, remains part of the space the viewer shares. The unification of the chapel puts the sculpture of the dying woman inside the space within which the viewer lives out the "fiction of presence"—a virtual reality in which Ludovica and what happens to her could just as well appear and happen to us. Bourgeois' recycling of Bernini, I contend, further elaborates and "invents" this attempt to unify sculpture and architecture into one all-encompassing virtual space.

Careri uses the model of montage as advocated by Sergei Eisenstein to explain the various aspects of this integration. Montage is for him a model for a unified viewing of disparate elements. It is, moreover, a dynamic model, a theory of reception. Cognitively, montage integrates iconography with the sensorial, thus producing pathos. And, most important, he insists, the "non-indifference of materials" makes for embodied form (1995: 5).

These four aspects of the montage model have recurred throughout my analysis of *Spider.* This is not to say, however, that

Bourgeois simply adopted what could be called a Bernini effect. Nor an Eisenstein effect, for that matter. Not satisfied with either influence or opposition, and shunning both imitation and mere polemics, "homage" means, primarily, taking seriously enough to engage with, from the inside. Homage is traversal here, as Lord (1999) would have it. It is inside Bourgeois' *Homage*, after all, that the tiny poles are polished to the point of becoming clothed in a baroque surface. Bernini, as theorized by Careri through Eisenstein, offers an appealing starting point for a reconsideration of what, thus far in my analysis, has been presented as a kind of montage of levels that moves from sculpture to architecture.

How, then, can *Spider*, with its mutilated *putto*, empty chair, and fragmented fabrics, relate to a marble religious sculpture? First of all, in spite of its classical medium—marble carving—Bernini's sculptures-in-chapels have famously been said to embody the "unity of the visual arts" (Lavin 1980). I contend that *Spider* relates to Bernini's holy women by way of its own theorizing. Bourgeois does not follow Bernini, despite what her sculpture's title *Homage to Bernini* might suggest; she beckons him. The theoretical contribution, here—and the one most significant as a revisionist proposition to art history as a whole—is condensed in this gesture. "Beckoning Bernini" is the performance of an intervention into historical looking. In my own response to Bourgeois' work and to *Spider* in particular, then, I propose this gesture as the lesson art criticism and history must draw from an engagement with this work on its own terms.

This historical attitude also works within Bourgeois' own oeuvre. Take one look at that sculpture from 1967, *Homage to Bernini* (fig. 20), which preceded *Spider* by thirty years. Roughly egg-shaped, but with one side caved in, it might be considered the spider's egg that bred *Spider*. Significantly, the sculptor, who with works such as

Cumul I amply demonstrated her interest in producing baroque marble surfaces, has chosen, as her homage to the master of baroque marble, to cast the work in bronze. No polished surfaces, no white smoothness waiting to be caressed. Instead, this work turns Bernini's painterly surfaces inside-out. Here, there is no separate layer of bark; the object *is* bark, just as coarse, but solid, massive. There is no inner wood that it hides. Yet the object is not entirely solid; it is also hollow. And inside, where you least expect it, is a tiny bit of Berninesque smoothness. Multiple, like the master's folds; but then again, inside-out. No suggestion of hollowness in these little protrusions. And, in terms of genitals (covered in *Daphne* or iconically aggrandized in *Ludovica*), this sculpture blows this body part out of proportion—literally. It is nowhere, or everywhere.

If *Homage to Bernini* can be said to have laid an egg for *Spider,* it foreshadows or projects—in a gesture against anteriority—*Spider* as a radically new work, one that does not, not at all in fact, "resemble" it. Instead, seen from the present, *Homage* becomes a spider egg that beckons Bernini from across the thresholds of modern sculpture's passages through time:[7] the time of history, which doesn't only move forward; the time of narrative, which is constantly interrupted and remains incomplete. Both temporalities hold the past up like a carrot that can never be reached; nor reconstructed or eaten and excreted; nor seen or eliminated. But, like such lures, the past is located in front of, not behind, the present.

The time Bourgeois deploys in order to confuse the illusory linearity and regularity of the time of history and narrative is the

7. This formulation refers to Rosalind Krauss' title (1977). Hereafter, if only because of its status within art history, I take Krauss' study as the paradigm of modern sculpture, to which Bourgeois responds but to which she does not in any simple sense belong.

time of architecture. I don't mean the time it takes to make a building, or to contemplate one, or the time it takes for the building to become a ruin of fragments that can never become whole again but only a hole. The architecture of Bourgeois' *Cells,* in a manner comparable to, though more radical than, that of Bernini's women-chapels, requires a temporality of *inhabitation.* As Bourgeois inhabits Bernini by inhabiting the tradition of sculpture in Western culture—from which she cannot be excluded yet in which there is no neat niche that can contain her—she inhabits his work in the mode of parasite. Over time, inhabiting inevitably builds a new logic, invents a host that did not exist before the parasite came to live in and on him.[8] In Lynn's words: "A parasite does not attack an already existing host but invents a host by configuring disparate systems into a network within which it becomes an integral part" (1993: 62). The shape of *Homage to Bernini,* with its smooth forms inside and its roughness outside, emerges as a model for this theoretical principle.

In its gesture of beckoning, this open, egg-shaped, early work breeds the position of *Spider* as the intersection of Bourgeois' two recent series, themes, or obsessions, of *Spiders* and *Cells,* which rethink the place of narrative on the one hand and the place of architecture on the other—*in,* not *around,* sculpture. This is how *Spider* "thinks" sculpture as inherently architectural. Not in the Vitruvian tradition of perfect symmetry, but in the baroque tradition of wavering scale, coalescing monads or cells, and infinite folds. Indeed, the baroque's primary figure, its figuration and mathematically precise metaphor, is the *fold,*[9] folds like the ones Bernini uses to shift from microscopically small figurations of ecstasy to the macrocosm of the chapel. The coexistence of outside

8. Michel Serres made the parasite an emblem of innovation from within (1982: 35).

9. See Deleuze 1993 and, for an account of the fold in contemporary art, Bal 1999.

contemplation and inside participation that the baroque sculptor could only achieve side by side, becomes, in an age of virtual reality, a renewed possibility for exploration.

Put briefly: the stories inhabit the *Cells,* which in turn are their performances. Inside, on that stage of cellular drama that has no director, only an empty director's chair, the stories constitute the cells inside them, which grow and pullulate, producing unpredictable shapes, destroying the unity, and emptying out the center. But the stories can only live inside those spaces, inside *Spider's* cage, if they are given life—time, subjectivity, body—from the outside.

Bourgeois' response to Bernini's search is perhaps most clearly visible in *Femme-Maison* (fig. 24), which belongs to another series of related works called *Femme-Maison.* In numerous drawings and sculptures over a number of years, the artist produced the semi-transfiguration of a female figure into a house which both imprisons and inhabits her body. Many of these houses are square, rectangular, angular, in a nearly hostile way. But in the 1983 *Femme-Maison,* the most Berninesque work of this series, the hostile skyscraper voluptuously sinks into a royal robe of folds.

Unlike Bernini's folds, Bourgeois' folds refuse all tendency toward regularity. On one side of this sculpture, toward the bottom, where the base becomes sheer matter, the folds confess to the deception of their illusory infiniteness as surface. Elsewhere, they detach themselves from the interior mass, betraying the banal secret of Teresa's transfiguration. Here and there, they are knotted, turning infinite texture into inextricable confusion, liberation into imprisonment. The cone-shaped body remains a body, refuses to go up in flames or be elevated toward transcendence. Firmly fixed on a visible disk-shaped bottom, this body is as heavy as Ludovica's but it does not believe in miracles.

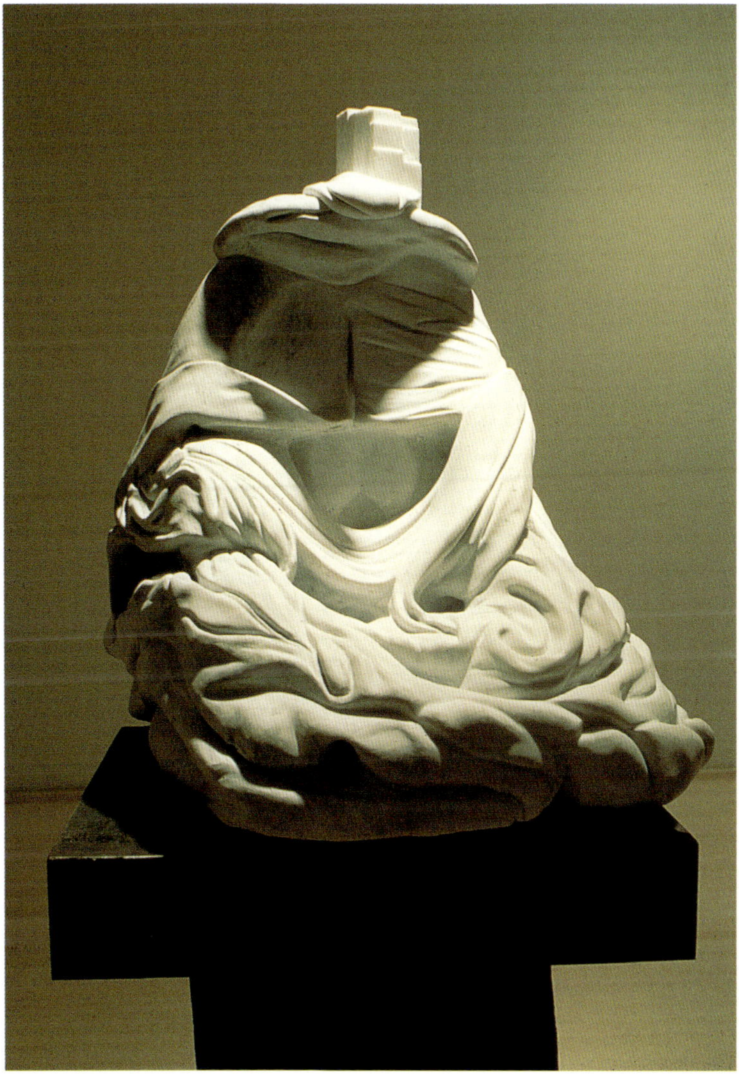

FIGURE 24 Louise Bourgeois, *Femme-Maison,* 1983, marble, 25 × 19½ × 23 in. Courtesy Cheim & Read, New York. Photograph: Allan Finkelman

On top, like a head, stands the angular skyscraper of twentieth-century architecture. The gigantic body of folds, and folds of flesh, that surround and incorporate this building, simultaneously state mutual dependency and threat. Like *Spider,* this sculpture absorbs architecture, in a secular, disenchanted, yet merry acceptance of the materiality of the body, the house, and the sculpture in-between them. A house in which women are locked up but also given mastery, a house that confines and protects, weighs the body down. But lest we escape reality by falling for transcendence and tragedy, the folds, knotted around the building as around the body's neck, are also just what they appear to be. Between figuration and conceptualism, Bourgeois winks at us, when, from one angle, the surface full of secrets turns out to be just a garment, lovingly warming the lonely house. Here the architecture encompasses motherly care, humor, and companionship—in this exploration of frightful interventions in space. In opposition to the Vitruvian tradition, this house-woman, while refusing the rigidity of classical symmetry, endorses the caprices of body and matter.

The level at which Bourgeois enfolds and then moves beyond Bernini is, then, one of the fullest integration of the arts. *Architecture* comes to stand for this full integration, this embodiment, that the house-enfolding body of *Femme-Maison* proposes. Looking forward from this work, we can see how *Spider* is fully architectural: not as a metaphor or as a literal building, but as a most literal acting out of the art of building. *Spider* makes good Bernini's promise to bring unity to the visual arts. Here, *Spider's* status as theoretical object is most fully realized. The preposterous historical responsiveness to Bernini's baroque effort at integrating the arts through architecture now receives its most profound completion—or might not "superficial" be the better word here, given the baroque refusal of depth and its more "profound" work with the fold. Except that "unity" is redefined, away from harmony. For the secret of its postbaroque success is the literalization of the one metaphorical term in Comas' Le Corbusier–inspired modernist definition of architecture, a term that contradicts the pursuit of unity: *debate* (1998). Bourgeois' work never tires of debating.

NINE

Passages through Modern Sculpture

But what if meaning, instead of preceding experience, occurs *within* experience? What if my knowledge of a feeling, pain for example, does not depend on a set of sensory memories but is invented freshly and uniquely each time it occurs for me? ROSALIND KRAUSS[1]

This continuous debating in her work is also the reason why Bourgeois cannot be placed in currents, movements, or periods. This is not to say her work cannot be considered historically. Among the sparring partners of her work as a whole, and of each piece individually, are, of course, also those that preceded it, within the orbit of its immediate past—sculpture in the twentieth century. It seems plausible to contend that it is in the sense that such categorization is impossible that her work is architectural. The architectural offers a way to engage with earlier sculpture but without integrating, because as soon as one tries to pinpoint Bourgeois' work in terms of any of the preceding currents, it escapes into architecture. Architecturality becomes her way of becoming friendly with her peers without marrying them.

As the paradigm of sculpture before modern sculpture as she construes it, Rosalind Krauss (1977) posits nineteenth-century relief. By deploying a historical nar-

1. Krauss 1977: 27–28. Krauss invokes this thought from Edmund Husserl (1859–1938) to position Rodin at the edge of modern sculpture.

rative within an illusionary space produced by a fixed relationship between figure and ground, relief sculpture as a medium, as she defines it, "links together the visibility of the sculpture with the comprehension of its meaning" (12). Thus the viewer is able to comprehend two reciprocal qualities simultaneously: "the form as it evolves within the space of the relief ground and the meaning of the depicted moment in its historical context" (12). To comprehend, that is, to see the one and understand the other. The sculptor functions like an omniscient narrator in a novel from the same period. The rationality of causality underlies the "natural" acceptability of such representations. Narrativity, here, is the opposite of architecture. Spatiality is entirely fictional.

But if narratorial omniscience is a key feature of premodern sculpture seen as antiarchitectural, Bourgeois and Bernini stand hand in hand on either side of that threshold. For the baroque sculptor *before* historical relief struggles with precisely the same issues as modern sculptors *after* that genre: to make seeing one act, to prevent splitting it up into the perceptual and the intellectual—into seeing and understanding—but also to make comprehending an act of integration of body and mind. Defying the ambition of omniscience, Bourgeois and Bernini pursue similar goals, albeit in totally different cultural contexts. Both use the instability between sculpture and architecture to pursue these goals.

Both sculptors build in limitations that saddle the viewer with compulsory efforts that counter any "natural" passivity in the face of representation. This obligation resides in the narrativity inherent in transformation. This narrativity must be performed by the viewer, who is invited to inhabit the architecture one cannot "penetrate." The "unity of the visual arts" that Lavin (1980) saw in Bernini's *Teresa*—but, significantly, analyzed in separate parts again—and that Careri (1995) theorized in terms of montage, by studying the transitions, the thresholds, rather than what lies between them, was not the ambitious project of Bernini alone. Bourgeois, standing on the other side of modern experimentation, develops, with the *Cells,* another attempt to rethink sculpture as the testing ground of what visual art in general can mean, or rather, in her conception, *do.* The *Cells,* and specifically, because of its uniquely sculptural spider and its scale in relation to the architectural unit it dominates, *Spider,* are no less than a discussion with both baroque and modern sculpture around architecturality. For the mediating term—the term through which this discussion can be conducted—is architecture. The *Cells* hold a conversation about the possibilities of a visuality beyond the cultural oppositions that have, literally, fixated the arts and the media in a confining place, where "sculpture" is studied, taught, and practiced in different departments and studios, and, conceptually as well as historically, understood separately, even by different "experts." For *Spider* militates against such cultural separations by means of its architecturality-within-sculpture. Like Picasso's cubist sculptures, *Spider* is visible from all sides, although the object—the spider—need not be decomposed in all its planes for that to happen. Instead of practicing cubism's analytical surgery on the object—its flaying of it—and within the acceptance of sculpture's temporality, the spider *is* all around the viewer. Bernini's *Apollo and Daphne* attempts to make the viewer part of its narrativity by allowing him to walk around the sculpture, but it fails in this because exteriority is maintained. Not so *Spider.* Both Bernini and Bourgeois decline to dissect the object for the sake of increasing the subject's visual mastery.

Like Brancusi's hyper-shiny objects that move and change with the light and the viewer's position, both artists' works destabilize the existence of matter in the world. Transformation, or transfiguration, is a matter, precisely, of matter changing, dissipating, and transforming: a matter of alternation. But where Bernini succeeds best in effecting such a transformation (when he turns a body into flames, then into pure levitation), Bourgeois opposes crumbling old matter, flat and fragmentary, to the Berninian illusion of representation, and to Brancusi's pristine shine.

Like Giacometti, Bourgeois and Bernini partition off a portion of real space.[2] Thus they overcome the dilemmas of sculpture: Is it part of real space? Does it occupy it, like a building? Is it a fictitious island that salvages some imaginary space from the drabness of reality? The answers lie, not in architecture as such, but in "architecturality." The suspended space of *Spider* is not quite fictitious, because the real viewer needs to enter it, inhabit it, so that she can partake of its creation as space. Instead of a fictitious space, then, we should speak of a virtual reality. The same can be said of what Bernini attempted in both his *Ludovica* and *Teresa.* But in Bernini's chapel this does not quite work, for if the chapel requires interiority in its architectural aspect, one still needs exteriority to its sculptural transformation. Only metaphor—Careri's "Flights of Love"—can help out here. With *Spider,* the distinction between inside and outside becomes moot; the sculptural space only works as such once it is also inhabited, as architectural. But the sense of inhabitation that architecture so often fails to accommodate is here literalized (by the chair, the open door), foregrounded "theoretically," by enforcing reflection on it—and only then, also metaphorically figured by the spider.

In surrealist fashion, Bourgeois defines the ambiguous space in terms of a double, entangled temporality. The time of the vicissitudinous encounter with the fragments is not constructed on

2. Krauss 1977: 114, 1999: 65.

causal logic. The fragments of tapestry, for example, do not obey an order of restoration, nor do they suggest a sequence of episodes forming a coherent narrative. The randomness is obstructed by the strong narrativity inhering in each fragment, soliciting each viewer to project his or her fantasies on them. Yet the fantasies are not quite left to the viewer; the fragmented representations bind them, as if critical of surrealism's illusion of "free" association's freedom. Bourgeois beckons Bernini as witness; one may give one meaning or another, painful or pleasurable, to the pressure of Ludovica's hand on her breast—hence, to the depiction of that clutching in Bernini's sculpture—but the female body remains immovably at the core of the fantasy. Looking at the sculpture preposterously, through *Spider,* it becomes clear that "core" is precisely what Bourgeois rejects, in agreement with minimalism's kinship with postmodernism; her fantasy-inducing fragments are obviously, visibly, materially, just surfaces. Walls, not bodies.

In talking about Jean Arp's sculpture *Growth* (1932), Krauss could be describing Teresa's transformative flames when she states: "Projecting a sense of fluid pressure from within the volumetric container, Arp's stressed surfaces become images of variability and change" (1977: 141). But *Spider*—although "speaking" of growth (with its fragments of natural scenery) and "performing" growth (through the very concept of the cell)—shapes change, not from the inside, where the cage is empty, but through the circling around that the viewer is compelled to engage in.

It is in relation to minimalism that Bourgeois' work is most outspoken in its friendly yet sharp, serious, and witty "discussion." Here, one would think, she stands alone, without Bernini. She agrees with minimalism's fight against preestablished systems. Nowhere in her work is there a systematicity that can be construed as anterior, as a priori. Even if the *Cells* use prefabricated construction materials—like doors, as in *Cell I* (1991), or window frames, as in *Cell* (*Three White Marble Spheres,* 1993), the most "minimalist" of the *Cells,* or even random units of woven steel—for their architecture, these materials do not reconfigure their function in the art of building. Instead, they signify it obliquely, hinting, through the existentially strong rhetoric of metonymy and synecdoche, infusing the work with architectural memory. But the repetition that embodies continuity is less emphatic in the material use of minimalist seriality than it is in the materialist pragmatic of the round shape that makes the viewer turn in repetitive circles. Like abstract signs, the *Cells,* although not at all abstract, refuse to represent. Instead, they address. They beckon.

As mentioned earlier, Krauss (1999: 54–74) reformulates Bourgeois' position between abstraction and figuration by shifting *Spider* away from a modernist logic of synecdoche. According to such a logic, the fragment stands for the whole. As such it is a refusal of "the narrative of gesture," a distillation of sculpturality to that part of the body that could powerfully stand for the whole. Needless to say, Bourgeois' play, in many of her works, with phallic shapes in order to de-phallicize them, challenges such a pure essence of the partial figure. Krauss moves the discussion instead to a psychoanalytically inflected interpretation of the body fragment as part-object. This is a successful move to counter earlier tendencies in criticism to consider Bourgeois' work as abstract. But it leaves the question of expressivity—begged by any psychoanalytic reasoning—entirely open. Instead of expression, of a pouring out of subjectivity, Bourgeois' work on subjectivity addresses the viewer. It is not a first-person account, of the analysand on the couch so to speak but—all Bourgeois' artist's statements notwithstanding—a second-person mode of interaction. She beckons, invites transference. Perhaps this strong invitation solicits criticism's enslavement to her prose. The empty chair speaks like a welcoming figure inviting you into her house.

For, like Donald Judd's sculptures, the *Cells* refuse expressivity. This alone should make critics cautious in their use of biography and artist's statements. The *Cells* refuse individual uniqueness. The fragments of tapestry are among the products of the earliest industrialized crafts. These fragments have no "authors." Yet, tantalizingly, they possess an aura of uniqueness. This aura is reinforced by the iconographic deceptions. A tapestry after Raphael only *appears* to be attributable to an author—to be individually authorized. But one does not sit in a Raphael or hang up fragments of one of his works. The integration of fragments of tapestry in *Spider* is a militant act that divorces uniqueness from individualist heroism. Their old age fleshes them out as materially—not individually—unique. They refuse to "express," to speak in a private language. The motifs on the fragments belong to an iconography so traditional that translating them into meaning is completely meaningless. They partake of a public language, bound to a class, bourgeois, sitting upon the furniture made by another class, the workers of the Gobelin factories. Even the fantasies and dreams they conjure up are, in a post-Freudian disenchantment, part of the public domain. Even when most engrossed in them, the viewer will not forget the public space she is standing in. And, even if a viewer were to risk dreaming away, the hard, unyielding spider leg behind her would make for a rude awakening. This edge, or lawn, between subjectivity and public space, which rehearses the minimalist attempt to oppose expressivity through restrained, meaningless form, is also the moment where sculpture tumbles into architecture. It is there, in other words, that a personal, "speaking" work of art is inhabited by someone who is not its maker and whom its maker cannot control.

For, perhaps even more radically than the minimalist sculptures whose tenets, if not forms, this work endorses, *Spider,* as I have argued here, brings the exteriority of public subjectivity *inside.* This is why the *Cells* are primarily architectural: they shelter. More effectively than the minimalist sculptures that remain confined to exterior effect, *Spider*'s exteriority, as a result of the enforced entrance of the viewer within the virtual domain between the spider's legs and the cage, and between body and eye, becomes interiority. More effectively because more bodily, the viewer's participation is comparable with Ludovica's levitation of body-and-soul, from between her legs to the folds that will carry her to heaven.

Like sculpture, architecture is an intervention in space. But architecture is more literal in its intervening. It does not allow fiction. Whether seen as occupying, colonizing, or structuring and delimiting space, territorial desire, rather than fiction, is part and parcel of the architectural imaginary. This is why it makes sense that, at the end of the day, Bourgeois refrains from *doing* architecture in the literal sense: she does not design buildings. But she does deploy architecturality as a language. This leaves the question of the implications of such a phrase: Does it add anything to our understanding of architecturality and of *Spider* to deploy the word "language" here? Visual art has a long history of exploring the different possible interactions between what Van Alphen calls "the representation of space and the space of representation."[3] It is within the framework of that exploration that Bourgeois works

3. In his lecture (Amsterdam 1998), Van Alphen discussed mainly painting and derived works of essentially two-dimensional visual art, from seventeenth-century landscapes and Carel van Mander's treatise on them to contemporary works that examine the relations between space and flatness. Van Alphen's theoretical argument is, however, directly and profoundly relevant for the architectural in Bourgeois' work.

her sculpture over with architecture. Rather than opting for building as her art, she explores representation and space in terms of both arch-shelter and intervention in space through fiction. Van Alphen distinguishes three kinds of representational spaces that

> can be acted out or activated in representation. First, the space in or behind the picture surface, the so-called depth of illusionistic space. Second, the two-dimensional space of the picture surface itself. Third, the "lived" space of the beholder, which includes her body, as well as the space in between the image and the viewer.

He convincingly argues that in contemporary painting, the illusionistic concern with depth leads in the direction of landscape, whereas the preoccupation with the flatness of surface leads to architecture. This is why, he writes, even Cézanne's still lifes of apples and Picasso's *Demoiselles d'Avignon* have an architectural look. *Spider* comes to these possibilities as it were, from the other end.

Van Alphen's interpretation of flatness as architectural seems paradoxical, since architecture was also a favorite testing ground for the exercise of perspective.[4] For, obviously, architecture is also emphatically three-dimensional. But in this view, architecture raises walls—obstacles. The point of Van Alphen's argument is that none of these distinct deployments of space are ultimately tenable. Rather, as he argues through a discussion of contemporary artist Marien Schouten's artistic project, there is a tension—which can take different shapes and engage different issues—between "illusionistic three-dimensional space, the two-dimensional space of the picture surface, and the space of the real viewer, again three-dimensional." The space of landscape lures you, whereas architectural space raises obstacles that stop you, de-

4. For example, the cityscapes of Urbino, as discussed by Damisch (1994).

manding respect for its territory, raising a wall between its territory and the viewer's. The effects differ because the relationship between the viewer and the object of vision differs. The wall has a door. But the inhabitant holds the key. In *Spider,* the tapestry fragments *are* the walls they decorate. But it is not primarily their physical opacity that imposes the architectural obstacle of flatness. It is their narrative allure. They claim architectural status so that they can invite the viewer in and slow that entrance down. In this temporal bossiness, this particular *Cell* enacts an integration of all three representational spaces that Van Alphen analyzes. No wonder the key dangles tantalizingly in front of you while the door stands ajar, almost open but not quite.

In *Spider,* I contend, this tension makes a case for the passage through both baroque and modern sculpture, and through painting for that matter, to an architectural sculpture whose terms have been transformed by that passage. A hint of this can be seen in the iconography, worn as it is, of the tapestries. The references to perspectival architecture in the *trompe l'oeil* paintings that are, as a genre, represented in that one fragment, and the representations of flowers, plants, bits of landscape in another, throw us off balance between one represented spatiality and the other. They clash when the only thing the eye is lured into is holes. Moreover, all the represented architecture is an obstacle unto itself. For the fragments stubbornly remain just fragments, although they are also the material obstacles that prevent us from rushing into the cage. And, as I have argued above, they are both narrative lures *and* obstacles. Seducing, then frustrating the viewer eager for stories, they are the temporal devices that slow down vision—but beyond a modernist, purist standstill.

TEN

. . . a monumentality that can do without permanence and without destruction, that is fundamentally informed by the modernist spirit of a fleeting and transitory epiphany, but which is no less memorable or monumental for that. ANDREAS HUYSSEN[1]

Hyperbole as Wink

In its debate with both baroque and modern sculpture, a debate in which architecturality is her language, then, Bourgeois' *Spider* maintains a very special tone. It is a tone that, in spite of the heaviness of the spider's thick legs as imposing body, also keeps alive a humorous lightness of being that makes all the serious, heavy, fundamental debate bearable, and more than that, attractive, fun. The attraction is an indispensable part of the "argument" this theoretical object is making. The tone refuses the earnestness that entails one-sidedness; hence the multiple possibilities of moods caught up in their variation, indeed, their transformation—from melancholy to laughter, from uncanny to witty, from fear to nostalgia. Why is the important element of humor in Bourgeois' work—the wink made explicit in Mapplethorpe's photograph of her—so underilluminated? Consistent with its vigilance against binary oppositions, the humorous element does not diminish the power of the theoretical object's posi-

1. Huyssen is citing Christo's Reichstag wrapping, which he calls "an event that was monumental and anti-monumental at the same time" (1999: 204).

tion. Rather it is one of the various media deployed in this (in this sense too) multimedia work. The baroque play with scale that implies excess in the unharmonious combination of huge and small connotes a deployment of hyperbole as a means of persuasion.

Rethinking sculpture as intertwinement with architecture: two radically different modes of relating to space must be brought to bear on one another. The difficulty yet necessity of that intertwinement is literally signified in the constant wavering between miniature and gigantic, two hyperbolic signs of size.[2] The ambivalence toward narrative seduces us to participate in the experiment. Hence the sense of habitat that coexists quite well with the radical impossibility of accessing the cage, of occupying the seat of subjectivity, that has been imposed by institutional vigilance against the artistic project.

In one of Bourgeois' recent *Cells,* this impossibility can no longer be inflicted on the work. In *Cell (Twelve Oval Mirrors),* from 1998, the twelve chairs that invite the visitor, literally, to take place so that the work can take place, stand on the outside (fig. 25). Concave mirrors stained on one side duplicate the inside-outside uncertainty in their mirroring effect. They pivot, so that the visitor is unable to politely refrain from touching the work. In one sense, the work emulates Bernini's montage of ecstasy inside the viewing space. The irresistibly baroque iconography of mirroring beckons to that historically remote time. In another sense, its insistent nonexpressivity nods to this century's passages through

2. Alex Pott (1999: 50) discusses a similar issue in terms of the wavering between close-up and overview. This is a well-known issue in experiential inquiry that goes back to modernist thought. See Bachelard 1927. Proust insists almost obsessively on the subsequent impossibility of achieving perfect perception (Bal 1997: 165–80). There, the emphasis is on epistemology; in *Spider* it is on cultural signification.

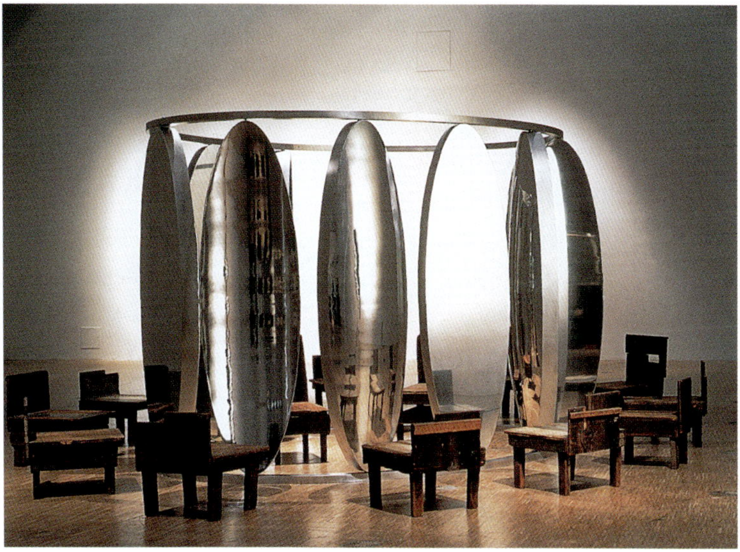

FIGURE 25 Louise Bourgeois, *Cell (Twelve Oval Mirrors)*, 1998, steel, wood and 12 oval pivoting mirrors, 96 × 132 in. Courtesy Cheim & Read, New York. Photograph: Adi Bereuter

sculpture. The scale of the mirrors in relation to the low chairs in which visitors take (their) place maintains the architectural thrust of the *Cells* as sculptural concept. But within the tradition of baroque *vanitas*, where mirrors are hand-held, the tall mirrors bind the viewer as inhabitant to the house that resembles her. All viewers, here, become a *Femme-Maison*.

That these mirrors are oversized is no surprise after the spider's columnlike legs. But if the gigantic is now deployed to mirror the publicly exposed subject, the sense of intimacy that is also part and parcel of habitat is threatened. If the *Cells* are to maintain the integration of sculpture and architecture (not a bypassing of the former in favor of the latter), the tension between protection and threat, safety and confinement, that pertains to the homebody that, in *Spider,* is the bodyhome, cannot be resolved in either direction. In *Cell (Twelve Oval Mirrors),* the darkened stains on, and the concave shapes of, the mirrors precariously maintain that tension. So does the incredibly delicate balance of scale—the chairs a bit lower, the mirrors taller than would be expected, together hovering between homeyness and hyperbole. In *Spider,* scale is also the means through which the rhetoric of hyperbole addresses the threats that make the architecturality of sculpture almost impossible.

Hyperbole is the rhetorical figure that signifies through excess. The effect of excess can undermine its "serious" message. When mechanically deployed, it becomes tiresome, sentimental, cliché-ish. But when brought to bear on the fundamental tenets of meaning production themselves, such as difference, time, materiality, and participation, each hyperbole transforms these from within. The one issue that so far has only been alluded to but that is perhaps crucial to understanding the deployment of hyperbole in this work also helps us come a little closer to understanding the concept of sculpture as architecture that this work embodies: monumentality. Wavering between grasp and overview is not just a matter of size. Beyond the epistemological dilemma involved, the issue put forward by means of size, in *Spider,* concerns cultural signification.

As has been argued, baroque sculpture and architecture—indeed, the unification of the two—was not only an historically important innovation in that it inaugurated self-reflexivity.[3] It was also an instrument in the literal spectacularization of Catholic power, indeed terror.[4] "Monumental seduction" is not to be taken

3. Erwin Panofsky made this point for visual art, in which the radical difference between caricature—mocking others—and irony—mocking the self—became possible in the baroque historicist awareness (1995).

4. The point was made with particular acuity by Michael P. Steinberg (1998).

lightly in the postbaroque, postenlightenment, and postmodern *Jetztzeit* in which *Spider* addresses us.[5] If we ignored the hyperbolic wink made by the spider's excessive size, we might well be caught up in an earnest-only reading that would bypass the work with scale in this recycling of baroque thought.

But, to avert the danger of monumental seduction, *Spider* considers, debates, the possibility of being monumental. A monument, writes Comas (1998: 4), is

> a machine for remembrance, a structure which endures against time and in doing so publicizes and recalls ideas, people, events, beliefs that are in some way out of the ordinary. Often associated with rituals whose formality is paramount, a monument is not identical with a landmark, but in order to function as a monument a building must be a landmark, it must be memorable. Memorability is facilitated by a certain degree of formal abstraction, by extraordinary size and scale, by a rather grave physiognomy and also by extraordinary richness of ornamentation.

He goes on to mention association with other monuments from the past as a contribution to defining a monument. To understand how *Spider* as *Cell* evokes, then rejects, monumentality, this definition is helpful. It spells out how Bourgeois triggers memories but declines to specify them as public; how she recalls the richness of ornament but tears it to fragments; how she recalls Catholic hysteria but winks at it; how she undermines the "grave physiognomy" of the thick legs through the lively dancing points; and how she deconstructs the narratives of grandeur that this definition of monumentality, like Bryson's definition of narrative, puts at the heart of the monumental.

If sculptural architecture or architectural sculpture is potentially and dangerously able to seduce people into bowing to naked

5. Andreas Huyssen gave this title to a critical analysis of contemporary monumentalist tendencies in Germany (1999).

power, it is because scale humbles the viewer and strikes him dumb, into heartfelt obedience. *Spider* recalls this danger. The sheer size makes it impossible to forget what can happen to subjectivity when it is physically intimidated. On the level of realistic representation, it matters that the object of representation is this small, humble, homely creature—a spider. On the level of *Jetztzeit* (my word here, to summarize, through Benjamin, the primary effectivity of this work in engaging the viewer in the act of viewing, each time anew), it is the excess of its size that helps to overcome—by working through—the dangers of monumentality.

On this level of signification, the shape of the spider becomes specifically relevant. The tall legs are thick due to their function as columns in the architectural "debate" achieved through their hyperbolic scale. But they end in fine points, barely touching the ground. This gives the spider, literally, a lightness of being, in spite of its humungous size. The tall and thick legs are columns supporting a building they also decorate. But the ballerina points of the legs, dancing around us, casting operatic moving shadows of great elegance as we walk around the cage, undermine, again literally, the now striking heaviness of the thick guardians they support. As we recede, after the long, sticky time of viewing myopically, peering in to see the perfume bottles and feeling our own body change scale, and almost hitting one of those legs, we recede farther and the spider remains where it is. Mute, cozy now perhaps, not intimidating—because its size was, after all, hyperbolic. This is what makes *Spider* effective in conveying, persuading, making us experience experience itself on all levels of the intellectual, the aesthetic, the mind, and the body—as individuals and as cells.

Outer layers are not, as Bernini already proclaimed, distinguishable from inner states. The perfectly smooth surface that makes marble look like flesh so that our eye can caress the stone's skin and feel its warmth is *Ludovica*'s hyperbolic program of sculpture. By making the spider more exterior than the outer folds of drapery but its egg-laying body more interior than the viewer's place inside the chapel-as-cage, *Spider* turns Bernini's sculptural architecture inside out. But even that (this unreliability of our senses to tell us where our body ends and the body of others begins) is hyperbolically made to affect us: in body (visually, but in a revised visuality) and intellectually (but through a theoretical object that speaks through the senses).

It speaks, that is, in a *Jetztzeit,* in which the sculpture as forbidden home tells itself through me. This is how *Spider* offers a radically innovative exploration of sculptural narrativity, in dialogue with both modernism and the baroque. The tale ends in a building, but one that turns our ideas about building, literally, inside out. It does not accept, as Robert Venturi lamented, that "space is what displaced symbolism."[6] To counter such nostalgia, it is crucial that narrative without clear stories remains a powerful cementing force in this work. By the same token, this relationship itself, as a revision of the way we tend to look at art, rethinks historicism.

SO, IN ENDING THIS ESSAY, I wonder what *Spider* has meant, said, and done to me. Summing it all up in a "conclusion" seems inappropriate. Such a gesture would involve a reappropriation of the mastery that I, in the wake of this art event, have been compelled to relinquish. Any attempt to pull the threads together ends up in a renewed dispersal. Centripetal, centrifugal, back and forth: such is the movement *Spider* suggests or enforces. But all the same I feel compelled to look back at the trajectory through this

6. Venturi, Brown, and Izenour 1972: 99, quoted by Wagner (1998: 39) in the framework of a discussion on postmodernism in architecture.

work as theoretical object, to see if anything can be drawn from it as a provisional program for art-writing.

Indeed, since entering into the orbit of the gigantic spider already entailed a questioning of this work's status between a great variety of media and modes, a retreat from cultural habits became necessary. Most remarkably, the first item on any agenda that aims to account for a work on its own terms and in its own detail—description—turned out to be both imperative and impossible. For *Spider,* as a paradigm of all strong works of art, hovers between *thing* and *event.* Things lend themselves to description; events solicit narration. The two modes are at war with each other; together, in their mutual undermining, they proclaim not only the priority but also the ambiguity of the aesthetic between general and particular, between experience and objecthood.

The argument against anteriority narrative, so at odds with writing about and by Bourgeois is, I feel, not an imposition from a critic who has a longstanding quarrel with intentionalism. For while I do have that quarrel, I am also a narrativity junkie. In fact, these two positions as well as the tension between them became the motor of my engagement with *Spider* as seduction to narrative. In this respect, Bourgeois' work recalls old still-life paintings that fight against heroic hyperbole and the hybris of the subject as inscribed in history painting. In an age when the spectacular takes over and subjects us to the tyranny of visual overstimulation, the lesson in attention is important.

The point of *Spider* as *Cell* concerns the need to break out of the oppositions that rule our cultural activities: interiority and exteriority, body and mind, microscopic and macroscopic existence, sickness and health. If this work has any stories to tell, they are the emblematic stories of the undercutting of those cultural assumptions so massively invested in binary opposition. And they include the way in which motherliness and fear are not at all at war. Bourgeois criticism, falling into the trap of the authoritative discourse of authorship, has been systematically unable to notice and acknowledge this thrust of the artist's work.

One overly famous instance where the ambivalences that reign in relations between generations, and specifically, here, between the positions of mother and daughter, is the fragment of the castrated *putto.* As the work's statement on approaches to art, this case embodies the solicitation as well as the mistake of iconography. "Reading" the hole in the *putto*'s body can only lead to tragic misreadings of both the fragment of tapestry itself, already an incurable case of nonwholeness, and the mother's presence, in other words, the transgenerational interaction in works of art, which always stand in a timeline but are not reducible to a development narrative.

As a remedy for the myopic historicity involved in psychoanalyzing reading, *Spider*'s relation to the tradition of sculpture, specifically baroque sculpture, represented here by Bernini, is the work's version of what I have termed *preposterous history.* As in all the work's theoretical positions, inevitably this is the result of my own interest in baroque art as much as it is *Spider*'s doing. The point is neither to deny the critic's input nor to impute to the work more autonomy than the situation of viewing warrants. If *Spider* beckons Bernini to revisit his sculptural attempts to capture women's bodily engagement with the objects of their passion, that encounter requires the mediation I have attempted to perform. For, *Spider* proposes, the kind of historicity involved in viewing in the present is of such an interactive nature.

With this gesture of reaching over centuries to find a mate for Bourgeois' search, I wanted to alienate my readers from the near-dogmatic short-term historicity so firmly established in art history. Modeled upon the same oedipally tinted scheme that makes this insistence on the presence of the mother in realistic terms—the spider is, stands for, represents the mother—so problematic, comparisons between the contemporary work and its immediate predecessors must be reenvisioned. The tendency to make such comparisons as well as the necessary failure to carry them through is *Spider*'s theoretical contribution to the immanent history of art. Finally, *Spider* stipulates that its play with and against monumentality addresses modes of signification that make works of art powerful as cultural agents.

Looking back, then, to a time when art was, much more clearly than today, part and parcel of political life, such as Bernini's work was for the Catholic church, is a way of reinvesting *Spider,* as an allegory of its own theoretical positions, with cultural striking force. This is why it is important, I submit, not only to recognize but also to participate in the way *Spider* demonstrates how, across a broken and two-way timeline, Bourgeois beckons Bernini.

BIBLIOGRAPHY

Alberts, Bruce, et al. 1989. *Molecular Biology of the Cell.* 2d ed. New York: Garland.

Alpers, Svetlana. 1984. *The Art of Describing: Dutch Art in the Seventeenth Century.* Chicago: University of Chicago Press.

Alphen, Ernst van. 1992. *Francis Bacon and the Loss of Self.* London: Reaktion Books; Cambridge: Harvard University Press.

———. 1997. *Caught by History: Holocaust Effects in Contemporary Art, Literature, and Theory.* Stanford: Stanford University Press.

———. 1998. "The Representation of Space and the Space of Representation." Lecture, Amsterdam.

Altieri, Charles. 1984. "An Idea and Ideal of a Literary Canon." In *Canons,* ed. Robert von Hallberg, 41–64. Chicago: University of Chicago Press.

Askew, Pamela. 1990. *Caravaggio's "Death of the Virgin."* Princeton: Princeton University Press.

Austin, J. W. 1975 [1962]. *How to Do Things with Words.* Cambridge: Harvard University Press.

Bachelard, Gaston. 1927. *Essai sur la connaissance approchée.* Paris: Vrin.

Bal, Mieke. 1991. *Reading "Rembrandt": Beyond the Word-Image Opposition.* New York: Cambridge University Press.

———. 1994. "Scared to Death." In *The Point of Theory: Practices of Cul-*

tural Analysis, ed. Mieke Bal and Inge E. Boer, 32–47. Amsterdam: Amsterdam University Press; New York: Continuum.

———. 1996. *Double Exposures: The Subject of Cultural Analysis.* New York and London: Routledge.

———. 1997. *Narratology: Introduction to the Theory of Narrative,* 2d revised and expanded ed. Toronto: University of Toronto Press.

———. 1999. *Quoting Caravaggio: Contemporary Art, Preposterous History.* Chicago: University of Chicago Press.

———. In press. "Intention." In *Travelling Concepts in the Humanities: A Rough Guide.* Toronto: University of Toronto Press.

———. In press. "Dreaming Art." In *Psychoanalysis and Feminism in the Visual Arts,* ed. Griselda Pollock. Durham and London: Duke University Press.

Bal, Mieke, ed. 1999. *The Practice of Cultural Analysis: Exposing Interdisciplinary Interpretation.* Stanford: Stanford University Press.

Battersby, Christine. 1998. *The Phenomenal Woman: Feminist Metaphysics and the Patterns of Identity.* Cambridge, UK: Polity Press.

Baxandall, Michael. 1985. *Patterns of Intention: On the Historical Meaning of Pictures.* New Haven and London: Yale University Press.

Benjamin, Walter. 1969. *Illuminations.* Edited and with an introduction by Hannah Arendt. Trans. Harry Zorn. New York: Schocken.

Bernadac, Marie-Laure, et al. 1998. *Louise Bourgeois.* Exhibition catalogue, Musée d'art contemporain de Bordeaux, Centro cultural de Belém, Malmö Konsthall, and Serpentine Gallery.

Bloom, Harold. 1973. *The Anxiety of Influence.* Cambridge: Harvard University Press.

Bollas, Christopher. 1987. *The Shadow of the Object: Psychoanalysis and the Unthought Known.* New York: Columbia University Press.

Bryson, Norman. 1989. *Looking at the Overlooked: Four Essays on Still-Life.* London: Reaktion Books; Cambridge: Harvard University Press.

———. 1994. "Art in Context." In *The Point of Theory: Practices of Cultural*

Analysis, ed. Mieke Bal and Inge E. Boer, 66–78. Amsterdam: Amsterdam University Press; New York: Continuum.

Careri, Giovanni. 1995. *Bernini: Flights of Love, the Art of Devotion.* Trans. Linda Lappin. Chicago: University of Chicago Press.

Comas, Carlos Eduardo. 1998. "Modern Architecture, Brazilian Corollary." *AA Files* 36: 3–13.

Crone, Rainer, and Petrus Graf Schaesberg. 1998. *Louise Bourgeois: The Secret of the Cells.* Munich, London, and New York: Prestel-Verlag.

Culler, Jonathan. 1988. *Framing the Sign: Criticism and Its Institutions.* Norman and London: University of Oklahoma Press.

Damisch, Hubert. 1994. *The Origin of Perspective.* Trans. John Goodman. Cambridge: MIT Press.

———. 1997. *Un souvenir d'enfance par Piero della Francesca.* Paris: Editions du Seuil. To be published in English by Stanford University Press.

Darrieussecq, Marie. 1997. *Dans la maison de Louise/Louise's House. Hors catalogue.* Bordeaux: Musée d'art contemporain; London: Serpentine Gallery.

Deleuze, Gilles. 1993. *The Fold: Leibniz and the Baroque.* Foreword and translation by Tom Conley. Minneapolis: University of Minnesota Press.

Deleuze, Gilles, and Félix Guattari. 1984. *Anti-Oedipus,* vol. 1 of *Capitalism and Schizophrenia.* Trans. Robert Hurley, Mark Seem, and Helen R. Lane. London: Athlone Press.

———. 1976. *Rhizome: Introduction.* Paris: Editions de Minuit.

———. 1992. *A Thousand Plateaus,* vol. 2 of *Capitalism and Schizophrenia.* Trans. Brian Massumi. London: Athlone Press.

Derrida, Jacques. 1989. *Edmund Husserl's "Origin of Geometry": An Introduction.* Translated, with a preface and an afterword, by John P. Leavy, Jr. Lincoln: University of Nebraska Press.

Duve, Thierry de. 1996. *Kant after Duchamp.* Cambridge: MIT Press.

Felman, Shoshana. 1983. *The Literary Speech Act: Don Juan with J. L. Austin, or Seduction in Two Languages.* Ithaca: Cornell University Press.

Fer, Briony. 1999. "Objects beyond Objecthood." *Oxford Art Journal* 22 (2): 25–36.

Freud, Sigmund. 1900. *The Interpretation of Dreams.* In Vol. V of *Standard Edition of the Complete Works of Sigmund Freud,* ed. James Strachey, 533–621. London: Hogarth Press.

———. 1910. "Leonardo da Vinci and a Memory of his Childhood." SE XIII: 59–137.

Genette, Gérard. 1981. "Frontiers of Narrative." *Figures of Literary Discourse,* 127–44. Trans. Alan Sheridan. New York: Columbia University Press.

Gorovoy, Jerry. 1998/99. "Standing on the Circumference of Roni Horn's 'Asphere.'" *Parkett* 54: 47–52.

Gorovoy, Jerry, Pandora Tabatabai Asbaghi, and Paulo Herkenhoff. 1997. *Louise Bourgeois: Blue Days and Pink Days.* Milan: Fondazione Prada.

Grootenboer, Hanneke. 1999. "Towards a Non-Perceptual Mode of Looking: Lacan, Merleau-Ponty, and Trompe l'Oeil Painting." Ph.D. diss., University of Rochester Program in Visual and Cultural Studies.

Herrmann Fiore, Kristina, ed. 1997. *Apollo e Dafne del Bernini nella Galleria Borghese.* Milan: Silvana Editoriale.

Huyssen, Andreas. 1999. "Monumental Seduction." In *Acts of Memory: Cultural Recall in the Present,* ed. Mieke Bal, Jonathan Crewe, and Leo Spitzer, 191–207. Hanover: University Press of New England.

Irigaray, Luce. 1985. *Speculum of the Other Woman.* Trans. Gillian C. Gill. Ithaca: Cornell University Press.

———. 1985. *This Sex Which Is Not One.* Trans. Catherine Porter and Carolyn Burke. Ithaca: Cornell University Press.

Keller, Evelyn Fox. 1995. *Refiguring Life: Metaphors of Twentieth-Century Biology.* New York: Columbia University Press.

———. 1999. "The Finishing Touch." In *The Practice of Cultural Analysis:*

Exposing Interdisciplinary Interpretation, ed. Mieke Bal, 29–43. Stanford: Stanford University Press.

Kotik, Charlotta. 1994. "The Locus of Memory: An Introduction to the Work of Louise Bourgeois." In *Louise Bourgeois: The Locus of Memory, Works 1982–1993,* ed. Charlotta Kotik, Terrie Sultan, and Christian Leigh, 12–28. Brooklyn: Brooklyn Museum and Abrams.

Krauss, Rosalind E. 1977. *Passages in Modern Sculpture.* Cambridge: MIT Press.

———. 1990. *Le photographique. Pour une théorie des écarts.* Trans. Marc Bloch and Jean Kempf. Paris: Macula.

———. 1993. *The Optical Unconscious.* Cambridge: MIT Press.

———. 1999. *Bachelors.* Cambridge: MIT Press.

Lacan, Jacques. 1975. *Le Séminaire, Livre XX, Encore.* Paris: Editions du Seuil

Laplanche, J., and J. B. Pontalis. 1973. *The Language of Psychoanalysis.* Trans. Donald Nicholson-Smith. New York: Norton.

Lauretis, Teresa de. 1987. "The Violence of Rhetoric." In *Technologies of Gender: Essays on Theory, Film, and Fiction.* Bloomington: Indiana University Press.

Lavin, Irving. 1980. *Bernini and the Unity of the Visual Arts.* New York: Pierpont Morgan Library and Oxford University Press.

Lord, Catherine. 1999. *The Intimacy of Influence: Narrative and Theoretical Fictions in the Works of George Eliot, Virginia Woolf, and Jeanette Winterson.* Amsterdam: ASCA Press.

Lowenthal, Anne, ed. 1996. *The Object as Subject: Studies in the Interpretation of Still Lifes.* Princeton: Princeton University Press.

Lynn, Greg. 1993. "Body Matters," *Journal of Philosophy and the Visual Arts.* Special Issue: *The Body,* ed. Andrew Benjamin (no volume or issue number), 60–69.

Lyotard, Jean-François. 1971. *Discours, figure.* Paris: Klincksieck.

Meyer-Thoss, Christiane. 1992. *Louise Bourgeois: Konstruktionen für den freien Fall/Designing for Free Fall.* Zurich: Ammann Verlag.

Mitchell, Juliet, and Jacqueline Rose, eds. 1982. *Feminine Sexuality: Jacques Lacan and the École Freudienne.* Trans. Jacqueline Rose. London: Macmillan.

Mitchell, W. J. T. 1985. *Iconology: Image, Text, Ideology.* Chicago: University of Chicago Press.

Morse, Margaret. 1998. *Virtualities: Television, Media Art, and Cyberculture.* Bloomington: Indiana University Press.

Muller, John P., and William J. Richardson. 1988. *The Purloined Poe: Lacan, Derrida, and Psychoanalytic Reading.* Baltimore: Johns Hopkins University Press.

Nemiroff, Diana. 1991. *Jana Sterbak: States of Being/Corps à Corps.* Ottawa: National Gallery of Canada.

Neri, Louise. 1998. "Effets personnels d'une femme sans secrets" (The personal effects of a woman with no secrets). In *Louise Bourgeois,* 73–88. Exhibition catalogue, Musée d'art contemporain de Bordeaux, Centro cultural de Belém, Malmö Konsthall, and Serpentine Gallery.

Nixon, Mignon. 1999. "Eating Words." *Oxford Art Journal* 22 (2): 55–70.

O'Toole, Michael. 1995. *The Language of Displayed Art.* London: Leicester University Press.

Ovid (Publius Ovidius Naso). 1994 [1916]. *Metamorphoses: Books 1–8.* With an English translation by Frank Justus Miller, revised by G. P. Goold. Cambridge: Harvard University Press.

Panofsky, Erwin. 1995. "What Is Baroque?" In *Three Essays on Style,* ed. Irving Lavin, with a Memoir by William S. Heckscher, 17–90. Cambridge: MIT Press.

Perlove, Shelley Karen. 1990. *Bernini and the Idealization of Death: The Blessed Ludovica Albertoni and the Altieri Chapel.* University Park: Pennsylvania State University.

Pollock, Griselda. 1999. "Old Bones and Cocktail Dresses: Louise Bourgeois and the Question of Age." *Oxford Art Journal* 22 (2): 71–100.

Potts, Alex. 1999. "Louise Bourgeois—Sculptural Confrontations." *Oxford Art Journal* 22 (2): 37–54.

Pranger, M. B. 1997. "Images of Iron: Communication and Dislocation in Ignatius of Loyola and Joyce." Lecture at Religion and Media conference, Paris, 12–14 December 1997.

Rajchman, John. 1998. "Jean-François Lyotard's Underground Aesthetics." *October* 86 (Fall): 3–18.

Roth, Michael S. 1992. "The Time of Nostalgia: Medicine, History and Normality in Nineteenth-Century France." *Time and Society* 1 (2): 271–86.

Scribner, Charles, III. 1991. *Gianlorenzo Bernini.* New York: Abrams.

Serres, Michel. 1968. *Le système de Leibniz et ses modèles mathématiques.* Vol. I: *La communication.* Paris: Presses Universitaires de France.

———. 1982a. *The Parasite.* Trans. Lawrence R. Schehr. Baltimore: Johns Hopkins University Press.

———. 1982b. *Hermes: Literature, Science, Philosophy,* ed. Josué V. Harari and David F. Bell. Baltimore: Johns Hopkins University Press.

Steinberg, Michael P. 1998. "The Materiality of the Baroque." In *ASCA Brief 1997: Intellectual Traditions in Movement* (ASCA Yearbook), ed. Mieke Bal, et al., 179–89. Amsterdam: ASCA Press.

Stewart, Susan. 1984. *On Longing: Narratives of the Miniature, the Gigantic, the Souvenir, the Collection.* Baltimore: Johns Hopkins University Press.

Stoichita, Victor. 1997. *The Self-Aware Image: An Insight into Early Modern Meta-Painting.* Cambridge: Cambridge University Press.

Treffers, Bert. 1991. *Caravaggio: genie in opdracht. Een kunstenaar en zijn opdrachtgevers in het Rome van rond 1600.* Nijmegen: SUN.

Venturi, Robert, Denise Scott Brown, and Steven Izenour. 1972. *Learning from Las Vegas.* Cambridge: MIT Press.

Vidler, Anthony. 1992. *The Architectural Uncanny: Essays in the Modern Unhomely.* Cambridge: MIT Press.

Wagner, Anne. 1999. "Bourgeois Prehistory, or the Ransom of Fantasies." *Oxford Art Journal* 22 (2): 3–24.

Wagner, George. 1998. "This Crushed Lantern: Wallace Harrison and the First Presbyterian Church of Stanford, Connecticut." *AA Files* 36: 31–39.

Weigel, Sigrid. 1996. *Body- and Image-Space: Re-reading Walter Benjamin.* Trans. Georgina Paul, with Rachel McNicholl and Jeremy Gaines. New York and London: Routledge.

Wittkower, Rudolf. 1955. *Gian Lorenzo Bernini: The Sculptor of the Roman Baroque.* London and New York: Phaidon.